The New Rules Of

WEALTH

Dispelling the 27 Myths of Personal Prosperity

Ben Benson

Published by:
Sabel & Stone
London & New York

millionpoundbook.com
7lawsofwealth.com

First Edition 2009

Designed and typeset by The Charlesworth Group

Cover design by Richard Stockdale

Printed in the United Kingdom

ISBN—978-0-9563898-0-0

To Dora Virginia Evans

Sept 5th 1917-Sept 15th 2007

Who taught me to believe.

Credit, where it's Due. . .

No book is ever a solo project, and this is no exception. Thanks to all my friends at Sabel and Stone Publishing who made this project possible. Terry Adby for his input and advice in shaping the material. Stephen Brown for being so generous with his time on the phone and email. Barbara Hanks for proofreading on weekends! To my family for putting up with me not being there when I was supposed to be. To everyone who has been and continue to be committed to the vision of the 7 Laws of Wealth. And finally to Julia and Janis my diligent assistants . . . Thank You All.

TABLE OF CONTENTS

Of Money, Myths & Mindset

The purpose of this book is to make you think about HOW you think about money. Pessimistic or negative thoughts about money can create a self-fulfilling prophecy, and then wealth becomes impossible.

Our beliefs, we are told, are ingrained early in life and can have a profound effect on our behaviour. As money is the stuff of some powerful mythologies, many negative, it seems reasonable to ask whether money myths, and the often questionable morality they reflect, have generated within us beliefs and attitudes that could be holding us back, not just in our financial fulfilment, but also in terms of realising our potential as human beings.

Sociologist Robert K Merton first coined the phrase "self-fulfilling prophecy." He wrote in his book *Social Theory and Social Structures* that "The self-fulfilling prophecy is, in the beginning a false definition of the situation, evoking a new behaviour which makes the original false conception come *true.* " This specious validity of the self-fulfilling prophecy perpetuates a reign of error. For the prophet will cite the actual course of events as proof that he was right from the very beginning."

"A reign of error". . . what a fantastic phrase!

Merton's case explains that once something is declared as true even though it is not, the act of believing it ultimately makes it true. And there's no doubt he's right. Belief itself alters actions and behaviours. If the belief is a negative one, inevitably it will have a negative effect on behaviour. Significantly, the belief may not, at the outset, even be held by the person ultimately affected. Others can have a huge influence on how we think and act.

For example, a teacher takes a dislike to a new student and decides he is going to be trouble. Every incident in the classroom is subsequently blamed on that student whether he was involved or not. He receives no praise for anything he does no matter how hard he tries. Eventually the student loses confidence, gives up trying, alters his behaviour because he is hurt and angry and morphs into the boy the teacher expected him to be. He *does* start the trouble in the class and he *does* do poorly in tests. Years later, as the cycle continues he may end up in prison. His teacher sees it reported in the local newspaper and turns to his wife over breakfast, "I knew that boy was trouble the minute I laid eyes on him." This teacher will cite the course of events as proof he was right all along. But he will not realise that he too was instrumental in creating the outcome through his expectation of that child, and how it affected them both.

His judgement of the boy was enough to colour his expectations so thoroughly, and so powerful was the effect, that the boy eventually fell to meet those expectations. This is known as the Pygmalion Effect.

The Pygmalion Effect—the human capacity to rise or fall depending on expectation—is named after George Bernard Shaw's play *Pygmalion* where a professor makes a bet that he can teach a poor flower girl to behave like an upper class lady. The same idea is used in the 1983 Eddie Murphy and Dan Aykroyd film *Trading Places*.

Think about yourself for a minute. Are you experiencing a 'reign of error' in your financial affairs? Are you creating your own Pygmalion Effect? When it comes to money, what are your expectations and beliefs? And how do they affect your behaviour?

Whether you realise it or not you have expectations about money and your ability to make and keep it. And like it or not, those expectations may well be built on false beliefs that you have picked up over the years from your parents, media, teachers, culture, environment and religion. Many of them are inaccurate, yet you hang on to them with utter conviction. As a result, you change your actions and behaviour and create self-fulfilling prophecies about your ability to create wealth.

So, let's dispel some of these myths right at the outset. Money does not equal vanity, corruption nor evil. Money doesn't automatically flow to those who already have it and away from those who don't. And money doesn't take sides! Let's be clear on one thing, money is impartial, neutral and indifferent.

It doesn't care who owns it, hoards it or who spends it. It just reflects the values of those that have it.

Used properly, money provides the ability to fully experience life. It can give you choice, security and the ability to look after loved ones.

Money may not always be the answer to a problem, but it can often help. Burt Reynolds once said: "Well, I've been poor and miserable. I've been rich and miserable. . . Rich and miserable is better!" Even in the worst times of his life, Burt could see the value and benefit of the money he had created in his career, and no doubt this positive view was an important driver in his success. How people think about money usually affects their results around money.

Your ability to create wealth, therefore, is not primarily a consequence of luck or circumstance, but a consequence of how you manage your thoughts. A big problem here is that most of us have no idea what we believe about money, or perhaps more significantly, *why* we believe it. This mythology is so deeply embedded in our subconscious mind that we don't appreciate just what our expectations are and how they may be affecting our results. We often don't question our own beliefs, because they are not on our conscious radar.

But in most cases these un-questioned beliefs make it very hard to feel good and very easy to feel bad about all sorts of things to do with wealth. Which means we hardly ever win . . .

"Gonna change my way of thinkin . . . Find myself a different set of rules . . . ."

Bob Dylan

It's time to change the rules. It's time to take control.

The New Rules of Wealth is your guide to liberate yourself from the widely accepted mythology and inaccurate beliefs about money that exist, and seem to be so pervasive. Based on sound principles from my own work, the 7 *Laws of Wealth,* I encourage you to bring your mistaken assumptions out into the daylight, look at them through fresh eyes and take conscious control over whether they really represent your true beliefs about money or not.

Wherever your beliefs turn out to be negative, or just plain nonsense, The *New Rules of Wealth* will help you to re-evaluate and re-position your thoughts about money more positively and constructively. If you have been on the wrong road, and conclude your conditioning has held you back, *now is* the best time ever to turn things around. Only when you end your own "reign of error" can you begin to work towards achieving the wealth you deserve.

Inaccurate beliefs and the lack of a good plan are a recipe for disaster in any walk of life—wealth creation is no different and too important to overlook. This book is about taking that first crucial step toward the eradication of the erroneous beliefs, negative rules and conventional wisdom you've gathered over a lifetime from well-meaning sources that have, up to now, actively STOPPED you from getting what you really want.

Lose the myths and learn the new rules of wealth.

What do YOU believe about money?

In the following chapters, I'll systematically cover all the myths that I have come across in my personal experience and teaching in this area. But this book is not really about money. And things are not going to change if you just read passively. First you need an insight into what *you* think about money, so before you read on, do the following exercise. The results will provide an extremely important personal point of reference.

Read the statements below out loud and finish them by writing down the first thing that springs to mind. Make sure you are not inhibited by the possibility that other people might see. If you don't feel comfortable writing in the book, then write into a notebook. Once you have gone through all the questions, repeat the process two more times to see if there are any more ideas lurking in your mind about money. If you are continually asked the same questions your brain will answer differently every time. At first you'll say the things that are close to the surface of your thoughts, if you keep asking the same questions you will eventually get answers that are buried a little deeper.

Don't think too deeply about the answers and just note down whatever springs to mind naturally and you will get a pretty true and accurate impression of what you genuinely believe about money. You may not consciously agree with some of the statements you make; you may even be surprised by some of them, but make no mistake, on a deeper level you resonate with what you write down.

Money is _____

Money makes you _____

People with money are _____

People with money have _____

If you have money you are _____

Money _____

I'd have more money if _____

My father thought money was _____

My mother thought money was _____

Money causes _____

If I had money I would _____

To have money I'd need to _____

When I get money I usually _____

In my family money was _____

Money equals _____

If I could afford it I would _____

Having money is not _____

You will probably find you get on a roll with this exercise, so by all means add any others that spring to mind along the way.

_____

_____

_____

Looking at your list, make a note in the margin using a -, + or N. Go through all the statements and assign whether you think they are negative, positive or neutral.

I don't have psychic powers but if I did I would be willing to wager that you had more negative statements than positive. Probably quite a lot more! And the reason I know this is that if you had money you probably wouldn't be reading this book in the first place! But you are reading it, and most likely would like to know how to make more. And if that is the case then your mindset is almost certainly leaning away from wealth-generation. You may consciously say you want to create more money in your life, but the beliefs you hold at a subconscious level are effectively cancelling that desire out. It is these limiting beliefs about money that are actively holding you back from achieving wealth. This is sometimes referred to as an Approach Avoidance.

This exercise will help you to appreciate that you may have some limiting beliefs. As you read through the 27 myths, cross reference them to your own list to see if you have written something that indicates you believe something similar.

Money Is The Root of All Evil

Riches should be admitted into our houses, but not into our hearts; we may take them into our possession, but not into our affections.

Pierre Charron

The idea that money is the root of all evil is the mother of all money myths (and probably the grandmother too). It's been around for thousands of years so it obviously has longevity. If it hasn't made your list, I'd be extremely surprised.

Only one small problem . . . or maybe two. For not only is it untrue, it's also inaccurate. "Money is the root of all evil" has become such a cultural sound bite, even those that have never read the Bible will have heard the statement. Yet it's not what the Bible actually says. The Biblical assertion is that, *"for the **love of money** is the root of all evil" (Timothy 6:10).*

The true quotation emphasises that the LOVE of money (not money itself) is the root of all evil. Lose the "love" and the meaning of the statement alters entirely. Those who spout the resulting myth point to the major ills of the world as evidence of its truth. And certainly things like drug smuggling, people trafficking and other heavy crimes are often motivated by "the love of money." But, as always, the root of the evil lies within the perpetrators, not the money. And, in any case, there is plenty of evil in the world that has nothing at all to do with money.

Money is nothing but a means to an end. It is a great servant but an unforgiving and often cruel master. There is no doubt that when people put their desire for money above everything else, their moral compass is forever altered, and that can and does have disastrous consequences. But money itself is not to blame.

How do we know this? Well, there are many people who have made serious money and have found ways to multiply and share it. Having money doesn't make you a bad person—it merely amplifies what you already are.

I am reminded of the saying "in vino veritas" ("in wine is truth." In other words the more you take, the more truth you will reveal). We could say exactly the same about money.

The person who said money is the root of all evil just flat out didn't have any.

Stuart Wilde

Is philanthropy evil?

Andrew Carnegie, the man who effectively commissioned Napoleon Hill to write *Think and Grow Rich* (the classic treatise on individual wealth creation) was an extremely ambitious and, some say, ruthless man. His formative years were spent in poverty in Dunfermline, Scotland, and it was that poverty that drove him to better himself. His family emigrated to Pennsylvania in the United States, and his first job was a bobbin boy changing spools of thread in a cotton mill twelve hours a day, six days a week. He was just 13 years old.

Carnegie's love of money and deep desire to leave his poverty behind was not evil, it was smart. He used his own experiences to put fire in his belly, and Carnegie went on to be one of the richest industrialists of his day. He spent the first half of his life amassing a great fortune and the last half of his life giving it all away. He was passionate about education because he recognised it as the road out of poverty for anyone. He founded the Carnegie Corporation of New York with the mission to "promote the advancement and diffusion of knowledge and understanding" and the Carnegie Mellon University. He established libraries, schools and universities in the US and UK as well as pension funds for former employees. There can be little doubt that Andrew Carnegie was driven by money, and doubtless loved what he could do with the power and wealth he accumulated, yet he wasn't evil—far from it. He left an enduring cultural, social, educational and economic legacy on both sides of the Atlantic.

Man must have an idol and the amassing of wealth is one of the worst species of idolatry! No idol is more debasing than the worship of money!

Andrew Carnegie

In modern times, Bill Gates looks set to do the same. For years Gates has been named the richest man in the world, and together with his wife is now distributing that wealth through the Bill and Melinda Gates Foundation. In 2006, billionaire investor and CEO of Berkshire Hathaway, Warren Buffet, pledged to give 85% of his fortune away. Buffet, who has for many years been the second richest man in the world and also a close friend of the Gates, earmarked 5/6th of his fortune (an estimated $30 billion) for the Bill and Melinda Gates Foundation.

It is quite clear therefore that money has no more to do with evil than it does with good. Good and evil have everything to do with people and their values. If someone chooses money over love, friends and family, then that is a reflection of their values. Money is just the convenient scapegoat for an individual's moral vacuum.

Why is this myth so toxic?

The "money is the root of all evil" myth is damaging because it vilifies money. If you believe it, how can you possibly create wealth and feel good about it? If you believe at some level that money is evil, or that money makes you evil, then even if your conscious mind wants to make more money, your subconscious mind will be holding you back because, by association, that attainment would change you- would even make *you* "evil."

In this way this myth acts as a limiting belief against your attainment of wealth.

Money is the root of all excellence.

Louis E Bejarano

So, we need a new rule . . .

A more useful *and* accurate adaptation of this myth is this: "the LACK of money is a root cause of evil."

There is nothing inherently noble about struggle. Just a harsh reality. There is no automatic creative response, no romance (except in films and books), little fun, nor room for anything but worry and heartache. Poverty may be photogenic, but behind the image of dignified struggle, a lack of money leads desperate people down desperate paths. A mother without money may steal baby food to feed her child—is that act evil? No, but the fact that she finds herself in such a desperate position in a wealthy world probably is.

So forget the myth and look at the facts. Having money just offers you a better way to live. Taking action against a LACK of money, while maintaining your moral compass, can make you a more useful member of society, and also help you to achieve your dreams.

Look at all the charities in the world. I have yet to hear of one that didn't value a financial donation. Money can provide freedom, choice, empowerment, increased self-esteem, value and even the ability to express goodness. It can allow you to look after yourself and your loved ones. It also provides an opportunity to support those less fortunate and make a positive contribution on a wider scale.

The love of money? Well, that is something different altogether. Make money your god and you will have the devil of a job to stay in control. Expecting others to provide money for you without work or effort is crazy. No one owes you a living—it is up to you to apply yourself to the task of getting what you want. But there's nothing wrong in that, and if you make millions in the mean time, you will have the right to enjoy it and the choices it can bring.

New Rule of Wealth No. 1

The LACK of money is the root of all evil.

A Well-Paid Job Is The Key to Wealth

It is most unusual for someone to become wealthy by working for a rich man.

Carl Riblet

This is another myth that has a great deal of time on its side and was created to make us feel better about attending school. "Go to school, get good grades and you'll get a good job"—that was the mantra. It was used as we grew up to scare us into making an effort come exam time.

But let's step a little further back than that. . . . School as we know it today is a system of socialisation and indoctrination as much as education. Compulsory schooling was actually introduced in the UK at the time of the Industrial Revolution. Machinery was being developed that required people to operate it and "schooled ignorance" was considered better than "mass stupidity." The idea was simple, get the kids off the streets, teach them enough to be able to do a menial job and never give them any aspirations to do anything other than what they were told they could do. That way they happily slotted into poorly paid, difficult jobs working long physical shifts while the owners of the mills and factories became extremely wealthy.

In the US the first mission statement of Rockefeller's General Education Board was documented as follows:

In our dreams . . . people yield themselves with perfect docility to our molding hands. The present educational conventions [intellectual and character education] fade from our minds, and unhampered by tradition we work our own good will upon a grateful and responsive folk. We shall not try to make these people or any of their children into philosophers or men of learning or men of science. We have not to raise up from among them authors, educators, poets or men of letters. We shall not search for embryo great artists, painters, musicians, nor lawyers, doctors, preachers, politicians, statesmen, of whom we have ample supply. The task we set before ourselves is very simple . . . we will organize children. . .and teach them to do in a perfect way the things their fathers and mothers are doing in an imperfect way.

Don't be too busy earning a living to make any money.

Joe Karbo

Working for others makes *them* rich not you . . .

The fact is, the industrialists of the day including Rockefeller, Carnegie and Ford needed docile workers without ambition to secure *their* fortune. Compulsory schooling was the answer to their capitalist prayers. Getting a well-paid job however is not necessarily the answer to yours.

I think working hard and getting some qualifications is important if for no other reason to prove to yourself that you have a brain and know how to use it. School teaches us discipline and the benefit of hard work but to assume that it will give you a free pass to wealth—least of all as an employee—is a mistake.

Working for the tax man

For a start, even if you do get a great job paying hundreds of thousands a year or more you are always taxed at source. That means that the Inland Revenue will take their slice of your earnings before you are paid a penny. At the time of writing you are considered a high earner in the UK, if you make over £35,000 a year. If you do, then you have the privilege of paying a whopping (come to think of it, a staggering!) 40% in income tax alone. That means you lose almost half of your earnings before you are paid a penny. Excited yet?

Sure, there are people at the top end of big companies who are making millions a year but their wealth does not come from the salary they are paid, but from the shares they are paid as part of their package. In other words it is their investments that make them rich, and that is the same whether you work in a school canteen or are CEO of a global company.

Many folks think they aren't good at earning money, when what they don't know is how to use it.

Frank A Clark

Organisations such as Google and Microsoft, which found success and worker fidelity through a generous shares and benefits system, do offer employees of a certain level an opportunity to own stock and benefit from the corporate success. But this is still rare for the vast majority of companies and employees.

Instead, most people get by on a salary and, what normally happens with it is that as someone progresses up the promotion ladder their expenses expand to match. The car is traded up for a nicer car, the semi-detached house becomes a detached house and the holidays become more lavish. As a result, debt increases too and mortgage payments and credit card debt leave the person with about as much disposable income as they had when they started their career.

The myth then moves from "a well-paid job is the key to wealth" to "a pay rise will solve my problem." Both are myths and both will do nothing for your long term wealth and security.

Why this myth is so toxic

The reason this mindset is so dangerous is because you are always chasing something in the future. You're always running just to stay in the same place. You waste your life trying to get to the next place, rather than loving where you are and enjoying the new adventures life brings your way.

As a result you die in the red, having never really lived.

The solution

Robert Kiyosaki talks about the cash flow quadrant in his book of the same name. In it he suggests that there are four ways to make money:

- Employed
- Self-Employed
- Business Owner
- Investor

People usually cycle around the first three. If they stay as an employee, even a well-paid employee they are taxed before they are paid. Besides, well-paid employees are usually working ridiculously long hours for the privilege, so when do they have the time to invest? For those that get tired of having a boss, they may branch out on their own, but it's rarely any better. There are tax advantages, but they invariably end up working longer hours than they did before. Perhaps if things go well, a true business is created where the business earns money whether the individual that started it works or not.

The real wealth, however, is created by taking the money you do make and making it work for you by investing it wisely. Investors are the only real long-term winners in the wealth creation game.

So whatever you do, find a way to be in business for yourself and/or make the money you do make work more industriously for you.

By working for yourself, you are always the CEO of your endeavours. You can't be made redundant and you are in control of your own destiny. And of course you pay tax after expenses, not before! Wealth is rarely about how much you make but how much you keep and how much you invest.

I appreciate, however, that self-employment or starting a business is not for everyone. Plus you may actually love your job but just want to make more money. In that case you have to get smarter about what you do with the money you do make and try and find ways to increase that. The first stage in that process is to get some knew knowledge so you can get inspired about what you can achieve regardless of what you make right now!

New Rule of Wealth No. 2

Profits and investments are better than wages.

If My Parents Were Rich, I Would Be Rich

I would rather make my name than inherit it.

William M Thackeray

This myth provides a fertile breeding ground for the proverbial chip on the shoulder, and the ideal excuse for failure to create wealth of your own if you don't happen to have had the perceived advantage of well-off parents. The assumption is that wealthy parents automatically give their kids a start that makes it possible for them to create more money. Or they inherit a trust fund that sets them up for life. Or perhaps those wealthy parents would have at the very least taught them the mysterious 'secrets' that only the rich know about—giving them access to the Promised Land. In some cases there may be some truth in some of this, but . . .

The exceptions to the rule

Based on this myth, Oprah Winfrey, one of the wealthiest and most influential people on the planet must have been brought up by wealthy parents. And yet if you look into her history, Oprah was born to unmarried parents in Mississippi. Her mother was a housemaid and her father was in the armed forces when she was born. Oprah spent the first six years of her life living in rural poverty with her grandmother—the sort of poverty that required her grandmother to make her dresses out of potato sacks. Her grandmother may not have had any money but she taught Oprah to read before she was three years old, which made more of an impact on her life that anything money alone could have done. She went to join her mother at age six although it was still a very hard life. Today, Oprah Winfrey is a household name. She is an Academy Award nominated actress, media personality, magazine publisher, talk show host and billionaire.

Or what about Sir Alan Sugar? If this myth were true, then surely his parents were well off and were able to give him the start he needed to create his fortune. Yet if you look at *his* history, he was born in Hackney, East London—the youngest of four children. His father was a tailor in the East End garment industry and the family lived in a council flat. He made extra money boiling beetroot and selling it at a local stall. After saving up £100 he bought a van and started selling car aerials and electrical goods from the van. He founded the electronics company Amstrad in 1968, the name being an acronym for his initials—**A**lan **M**ichael **S**ugar **Trad**ing. At its peak Amstrad achieved a stock market value of £1.2 billion. Today Sir Alan Sugar is estimated to be worth £730 million and was ranked 59th in the *Sunday Times Rich List 2009*.

On the other side of the fence there are the Menendez brothers. On the 20th August 1989, Jose and Kitty Menendez were shot dead in the den of the family's 722 Elm Drive home in Beverly Hills. What made the murder so shocking was it was committed by the couple's two sons. Joseph Lyle and Erik Galen Menendez grew up in a privileged environment. They had everything and were afforded the very best education—but it apparently wasn't enough.

Although never initially suspected for the crime, their subsequent spending spree aroused suspicion. They spent $1 million in their first six months as orphans. Finally Erik confessed to his psychiatrist who told the police after being threatened by Joseph.

Erik and Joseph Menendez's parents were wealthy, and it turned them into murderers who can now expect to spend the rest of their lives in prison.

Are there people with wealthy parents who help them out or get them started in business? Of course there are, but just as many people who have never got a penny from their parents have gone on to create vast fortunes. I chose Oprah Winfrey and Sir Alan Sugar to make my point, but there are countless other high profile examples.

The best inheritance a parent can give his children is a few minutes of his time each day.

Orlando A Battista

There are also plenty of examples of people who have been given that head start and made a complete mess of it. To most people, Paris Hilton hardly seems a shining example of what can be achieved with inherited wealth!

Let parents bequeath to their children not riches, but the spirit of reverence.

Plato

The fact is whether or not your parents are wealthy is irrelevant. I've interviewed over 177 of the wealthiest self-made individuals in the world, and a tiny minority of those individuals were assisted by wealthy parents. More often than not the start-up funds were bootstrapped together through small entrepreneurial beginnings.

There is no secret information

Another layer to this myth is the idea that the rich are privy to some secret information, that they are in effect part of a covert society where wealth-generating secrets have been passed down for generations. This too is pure fallacy. There are no secret rules to wealth. It is true that there are laws that money follows and these are discussed in my book *The 7 Laws of Wealth*. But there are no *secrets,* and anyone that tells you otherwise is trying to cash in on your hopes and dreams. There is no magic bullet.

Why this myth is so toxic

Because it makes you lazy! It's a convenient clause that allows you to blame something outside of yourself for your own situation. When your head is full of half-assed myths like this one you can abdicate responsibility for your failure. But let's be honest—this isn't really a myth, it's an excuse. To blame family, fate and adverse circumstances for what you have not been able to achieve is a cop out and we both know it.

The solution

Decide now whether you're going to be a winner or a whiner.

Whether you like it or not, you ARE the captain of your own destiny. You have two choices: stay mediocre and wait for money to fall from the sky (AKA play lottery) or find what you will love doing most and create a successful business from it.

All this can be started in your own home. No fancy offices are required—just a solid idea backed with passion, creativity, guts and hard work. Everyone has the potential to make a shift in their relationship towards financial stability and independence. A few will realise it.

New Rule of Wealth No. 3

Wealth is not dependent upon genetics, inheritance or handouts.

Rich People Are Greedy

Money doesn't change men, it merely unmasks them. If a man is naturally selfish, or arrogant, or greedy, the money brings it out; that's all.

Henry Ford

This myth that rich people are greedy is a meaningless generalisation, like saying rich people all have blue eyes. It may be true for some but is certainly not a cast iron rule. Sure, some rich people may be greedy. But many are not. Some poor people may be greedy. But many are not.

"Greed is good"

Michael Douglas's character, Gordon Gecko, in the 1980s film *Wall St.* personified the city high-flyer image of wealth and greed. It's an image that has since stuck, and with the past global financial crisis it's hard to argue that Gordon hasn't been alive and well in corporations across the world. "Greedy" is also a word that springs to mind amidst the 2009 politicians' expenses row in the UK, where the great and the good from all parties were exposed for the excessive expenses, claimed at the public expense—light bulbs and food bills, even the cleaning of a moat!

But to cast the rich as greedy by default is an error.

Let's take Henry Ford for example—he was by all accounts an extremely wealthy man. He was also the archetypal hard-nosed businessman. In his book *My Life and Work,* Ford offers a disturbing insight into his view on the role of people in his organisation. He calculated that the production of a Model T required 8,882 different operations. Of these, 949 required "strong, able-bodied, and practically physically perfect men" and 3,338 required "ordinary physical strength." The remainder according to Ford could be undertaken by "women or older children" and "670 could be filled by legless men, 2,637 by one-legged men, 2 by armless men, 715 by one-armed men and 10 by blind men."

Ford was no humanitarian and yet in 1914 he doubled his workers' pay from $2.50 a day to $5 a day. These are hardly the actions of a greedy man!

They were, however, the actions of a smart businessman. In raising his workers' wages, he did two things. First he made it very difficult for them to leave. Those processes he was so keen on identifying were mind numbingly boring and his staff turnover was significant. Increasing the pay so dramatically went a long way towards solving that problem. In addition, he created a market for his own product. At $5 a day his workers could now afford to buy the Model T that they helped to create—therefore making the motor car accessible to the ordinary man. He also reduced the working hours so that they might have some down time to actually enjoy driving it!

After a certain point, money is meaningless. It ceases to be the goal.
The game is what counts.

Aristotle Onassis

Greed is short-sighted

The simple fact is that the rich, certainly the self-made rich, are rarely greedy—they recognise that greed, certainly at the cost of those who work for them, will backfire.

In Adam Smith's economic classic *The Wealth of Nations,* Smith noted that, *"There is however a certain rate below which it seems impossible to reduce for any considerable time the ordinary wages even of the lowest species of labour."* Adding that, *"A man must always live by his work, and his wages must at least be sufficient to maintain him."* Even the 18th century employers realised that extreme greed was detrimental to wealth creation. If workers were not paid enough, they would not be able to maintain their families, and their children would then not survive to enter the workplace. Like Henry Ford, they also realised that if they didn't pay well enough then they would limit the market for their own produce. Money only works if you keep it circulating.

Clearly the self-made rich can't afford to be greedy!

And besides, what is more greedy—a businessman who has worked hard to create a thriving business employing hundreds of people and happens to drive a hard bargain, or someone who has never worked a day in their life and yet feels it their right to exist off the welfare system? Greed takes many forms. And has little or nothing to do with being rich or poor.

My father said: "You must never try to make all the money that's in a deal. Let the other fellow make some money too, because if you have a reputation for always making all the money, you won't have many deals."

J Paul Getty

Why this myth is so toxic

This myth is damaging because it assumes that all rich people are rogues motivated toward wealth by their greed. Yet having personally worked with many extremely wealthy people, I found it's not the money that motivates them—it's winning the game that inspires them. They love the feeling of making a difference.

Truly greedy people, on the other hand, are totally self-interested. They are not even interested in playing the game—they just want the money for its own sake.

Believing this myth means that think that anyone creating honest wealth—even you—will be cursed to become greedy in that process. As such you will shy away from opportunities for fear that it will somehow corrupt you and make you into something to despise.

Or alternatively you will simply use this myth as an excuse not to even try.

The solution

As Adam Smith pointed out and Ford demonstrated, it's actually terribly difficult to make money if you're not generous. Money works best when opportunities to grow it are shared. While they may be very careful—astute even—in how they invest and where they spend—greed is a short-sighted approach to money and is rarely a characteristic of the truly wealthy.

Everyone needs to build and protect their earnings. In that respect everyone needs a healthy dose of looking after number one. If you can't look after yourself then how can you ever help others? If you are materially poor yourself how can you give to others and help them? Everyone needs to earn, and protecting your earnings gives you choices. That doesn't make you greedy—it makes you smart.

New Rule of Wealth No. 4

Rich people are often ambitious, But ambition does not equal greed.

Money Isn't Important

Money isn't everything. . . but it ranks right up there with oxygen.

Rita Davenport

Let's cut to the chase . . . there may be some people somewhere for whom this 'myth' is actually true. But you are not one of them because if you were you would never be reading this book! If money truly wasn't important to you why would you read a book called *The New Rules of Wealth?*

As you quite clearly are reading this book, then money does *matter* to you. You may not have as much as you want or you may struggle to keep what you make, but money is at least of interest to you. You want or need more, so therefore, money is important because nothing can really take its place.

You spend money on what you value

Wealth often comes down to values and focus. Our values determine what we spend time on. What you spend time on, what you do and who you spend your time with are all a reflection of your values. Your results are therefore a reflection of your values also. John W Gardner once said, "All of us celebrate our values in our behaviour."

Often those without money console themselves with this myth and say that love, family and friends are more important. They are correct in that regard. Love, family and friends *are* more important, and yet without money, all of those relationships can become unnecessarily strained and unhappy. Used wisely, money allows us to focus on what we truly cherish. But if you don't focus on money to some extent, then those people and things you cherish may suffer.

If you currently don't have money in your life and are always finding too much '*month*' at the end of the money, then chances are money is not something you value highly enough. If you were to write down the 10 things you value most in the world, my guess is that money would not feature in the top three.

If you want wealth, you have to focus on wealth. You have to make it important and make it a priority. Where focus goes, energy flows.

We all need money but there are degrees of desperation.

Anthony Burgess

Everyone needs enough

Ironically you probably need to have a certain amount of money to believe it is not important. Such people may not be wealthy but neither are they poor, so in that respect money is not a concern. They don't have to worry about it and have enough for their needs. Even for those people, however, money would become very important if there was no longer enough.

There's a significant difference between focusing on money to solve ALL your needs and challenges and neglecting the rest of your life and the things you value.

Money will never solve all your problems. If your relationships are poor now they may not be improved by money, and yet good relationships can be permanently damaged by lack of money. The strain can become intense, and even the strongest bonds can be broken by money. I have seen it time and time again. It is, however, not a magic bullet. But to say it's not important is akin to sticking your head in the sand.

Money is better than poverty, if only for financial reasons.

Woody Allen

Making money a priority doesn't mean you have to neglect other valuable things in your life. No one except the really wealthy can afford to be THAT busy that they couldn't divert a few hours a week to making money important. Remember, if your interpretation of this myth leads you to neglect your financial health, sooner or later money will be important!

Money is like a friend—if you don't treat it right, it'll go away. Treat it right, make it a priority in your life and it will stand by you and support you your whole life.

Why this myth is so toxic

This myth allows you to ignore the issue. You will tell yourself that money isn't important—even though you don't believe it. Or you will tell yourself that friends and family are more important, and you don't therefore have the time to dedicate to wealth creation without damaging those relationships.

As a consequence of not giving money greater priority, you never make time for wealth or educating yourself about how you could better manage the money you already have. You push it out of your mind and make poor financial choices, always comforted by the notion that you did it for the higher purpose of spending quality time with the people that matter in your life.

The solution

Focusing time and energy on making money does not have to come at the expense of family and friends. This is an assumption that can hold people back from making money a priority, and it's a bit of a fallacy. What about turning the TV off? Curtailing some of your leisure activities? Reading the daily papers to get financially educated, rather than depressed at how bad things are (or at least that's what they would have us believe).

You don't have to feel guilty about focusing on having money if your basic value system includes sharing it and the opportunities it creates to make a positive difference in your life and the lives of people you care about

New Rule of Wealth No. 5

Money is important. It's not everything, but try living without it!

Security Is Good; Risk Is Bad

If you risk nothing, then you risk everything.

Geena Davis

It sometimes seems we live in a world that perceives risk to be unnatural, and security the only goal. The myth that one is good for us and the other bad for us is closely related to the longstanding idea that if we did well in school we'd get a good job and the world would be fair to us. As well as preparing us for lifelong employment, compulsory schooling got us used to being inside institutions. We were told that getting a job offered us security and safety from the uncertainty of life (and perhaps with no danger of making any money either!).

The illusion of security

If you ask 100 people on the street whether it is "safer" to be employed by someone else, or to go into business for yourself, my guess is that 90% plus would say that employment was the secure route. When you consider the folklore that states that most businesses fail within the first five years—not to mention apocryphal stories of people who gambled everything, and lost—it's easy to see why people think security is good and risk is bad.

We are brought up believing it and the message is reinforced time and time again all the way through school and later in the workplace.

But let's take a moment to consider if it's true or not. I am writing this to the now familiar sounding news that all branches of a historic UK financial institution, the Cheltenham & Gloucester Building Society are to be closed down with the loss of 1500 jobs. Global unemployment is currently higher than it's been for decades. Recession is biting and as an employee all you can do is keep your head down, do the best job you can and hope to ride it out. Yet out of the blue through no fault of your own you may be out a job. Does that sound secure to you?

Or what about the millions of pensioners or early retirees who decided to minimise their risk and keep their accumulated wealth in supposedly safe financial institutions? In the UK they have seen their investments in banks and building societies decimated as interest rates dropped from 6% plus to less than 1% on savings. In the US, 401k's have now become 201k's. Does *that* sound secure to you?

There was a time that there was nothing safer than the bank. "As good as money in the bank" or "take it to the bank" to refer to an absolute certainty were phrases that demonstrated the security of banking.

Banking is a big money business, and banks have become extremely wealthy convincing ordinary people that security is good. The trouble is, as the current financial crisis has illuminated, the banks have not been taking their own advice. The reason the financial collapse happened in the first place was that banks eventually woke up to the fact that, while you were banking on them for security, they had been investing your money in extremely risky investments. Those investments started to go bad, and the banking world panicked. They stopped lending to each other as well as the public, and that caused the credit crunch, which we will be experiencing the consequences of for years to come. At the time of writing, the UK Government owns a hefty slice of most of the high street banks and has saved several, including The Royal Bank of Scotland, from certain collapse. A similar scenario has been played out across the world. It seems that, like risk, security can come at a heavy price.

Life is inherently risky. There is only one big risk you should avoid at all costs, and that is the risk of doing nothing.

Denis Waitley

Risk is part of life

Risk is a daily part of life—we just don't view it in those terms. When you jump into your car you are taking a risk. You have no way of knowing how others will drive or what conditions you will find on the roads. You have no way of knowing whether you will arrive at your destination safely, and yet you drive anyway because you need to or you know it brings a benefit. You take the risk. You pay attention to the traffic conditions, you choose routes that you know to have less traffic and you don't drive through notorious black spots. In other words you manage your risk and minimise the potential for error or accident through those conscious choices. Money is no different, only we have been conditioned to view wealth creation through the eyes of risk *or* security.

If you want to make big money it seems you have to take extravagant risks. And yet if you look at the most successful investors of all time, you will note that the very opposite is true. There's nothing reckless about Warren Buffet. His investments are calculated risks based on a set of rules he rarely deviates from. As a result he is by far the most successful investor of all time. Sir Phillip Green told me that he had never 'bet the ranch' on a new investment.

There can be something sexy about taking risks. At least that's how it is portrayed in the media. Hollywood has made millions out of portraying risk as attractive and exciting. Life on the edge. Yet Hollywood and real life rarely share any similarities.

But wealth creation is not principally about security *or* risk—it's about education and ignorance. Warren Buffet knows what he invests in inside out. He understands the market and what is likely to impact that market, and he allows for the unexpected. He is an educated investor. After all, you can't manage what you don't understand!

Life is all about risk, but risk doesn't have to be reckless. You might say there is good risk, and there is bad risk. It all depends on what's at stake, how important the reward for that risk is to you and what you can afford to lose. You don't always have to risk everything to get what you want. But you will have to risk part of what you have to get what is best for you in the longer term.

Why this myth is so toxic

The 'security good, risk bad' myth is toxic because it shuts your mind off to opportunities. If we are led to believe from an early age that security is good and risk is bad then we are unlikely to take even calculated risks to further our position.

And yet the evidence suggests there is no such thing as security anyway! When the banks of the modern world can no longer be trusted to keep your savings secure, then what exactly is "safe"?

The solution

Information is power. So, demand information. "What exactly do you mean that *risk is bad?* Who says so? Why did they say that?" "What are the risks involved in this decision?"

Work risks out for yourself. Challenge your assumptions, enable risk and security so that you can make educated decisions that best support your life. And remember the words of Robert Rawls:

It is the risk element which ensures security. Risk brings out the ingenuity and resourcefulness which ensures success.

New Rule of Wealth No. 6

Uneducated risk is dangerous— educated risk is opportunity.

Money Can't Buy Happiness

It is a kind of spiritual snobbery that makes people think they can be happy without money.

Albert Camus

The Easterlin Paradox is a key concept in happiness economics. It is named after economist Richard Easterlin who wrote a paper called *Does Economic Growth Improve the Human Lot?* Published in 1974, Easterlin found that although people with higher incomes are more likely to report being happy, the level of happiness does not vary much with national income per person.

His paper concludes, "In the one time series studied, that for the United States since 1946, higher income was not systematically accompanied by greater happiness." Although income per person rose steadily in the US between 1946 and 1970, average reported happiness showed no long-term trend and actually declined between 1960 and 1970.

More recently, Andrew Oswald of the University of Warwick, England, has taken up the mantle of trying to work out if money and happiness are linked. Oswald's research work concentrates on economics and social determinants of mental health and happiness. He concludes from his own research that, "There is overwhelming evidence that money buys happiness. People with wealth rate substantially higher in satisfaction with life than very poor people do, even within wealthy nations."

Oswald is not alone in defying Easterlin's initial claims that money can't buy happiness.

Real happiness is not dependent on external things. The pond is fed from within. The kind of happiness that stays with you is the happiness that springs from inward thoughts and emotions. You must cultivate your mind if you wish to achieve enduring happiness.

William Lyon Phelps

Happiness is relative

Happiness is a relative term of course, so assuming that money is going to automatically make you happy is a mistake.

Just look at lottery winners. There are countless examples of lottery winners who have had to move home because they were plagued by requests for money, or whose friends started to resent them. Many have quit work and found they miss the social interaction and the kinship of friends and colleagues. Their happiness actually drops. Then there are the extreme cases such as John McGuiness who won £10,055,900 in a £40 million rollover in 1996. At the time of the win he had split up from his first wife and was staying with his parents. In February 2008 he was seeking a council house in Scotland and was £2.1 million in debt. Money didn't make him happy—at least not in the long run!

Or what about Angela Kelly who became the UK's largest lottery winner scooping £35 million in August 2007. She turned into a virtual recluse. A neighbour reported, "Winning £35 million has really ruined her life. The pressure is just too huge for her to bear . . . She was perfectly happy before. Now it's as though she's lost her sense of purpose."

Clearly assuming that money will fix everything and make you happy isn't accurate. But there are some significant correlations.

Money is a terrible master but an excellent servant.

P T Barnum

Money can give you freedom, which helps to provide happiness

Happiness consists of things like freedom from financial stresses, the ability to be generous to others, the ability to pay for a good education for your family, to travel to far off places and explore the planet. Happiness is about being able to pursue your dreams and ambitions unencumbered by the need to do a job you hate just to pay the bills. It's about finding and creating material, emotional and spiritual contentment for yourself and others in a way that makes your life and relationships fulfilling and meaningful. Happiness is about being able to positively contribute and influence those you love and the wider community.

These are the attributes of happiness and there can be no doubt that they may be facilitated by money. Money gives you choice and freedom to choose your own destiny.

One thing is for sure—the lack of money doesn't make you happy! Being poor is never fun. It adds stresses and strains to an ordinary life as you struggle to make ends meet. There is no relief from poverty or lack of money, and if you live in those circumstances, the money you don't have is on your mind 24/7.

Money alone does cannot guarantee fulfilment. It can buy a house, but not a home. A bed, but not a good night's sleep. Education, but not experience. A wedding, but not a marriage. A holiday, but not happiness. But lack of money is a condition that usually comes accompanied by an all-pervading and often debilitating stress. If money doesn't buy you happiness, then lack of money certainly won't.

Why this myth is so toxic

As far as toxicity goes this one isn't that bad! You do have to separate happiness from money because they don't belong together. It's like putting a square in a round hole.

You have to find happiness in your life with or without money. But the evidence suggests that money gives you options and choices that make happiness more possible.

The solution

Money does not necessarily buy you happiness but it gives you choice and choice can buy happiness. No one enjoys struggling; it's no fun lying in bed night after night worrying about how you are going to pay the bills. There is no enjoyment knowing that there is never enough to look after those you love.

Pursuing your own financial independence therefore is a necessary part of a fulfilling, enjoyable life.

New Rule of Wealth No. 7

Money can buy you choice.

It's 'The Economy!'

In today's economy there are no experts, no "best and brightest" with all the answers.
It's up to each one of us. The only way to screw up is to not try anything.

Thomas J Peters

Boom and bust

Waiting for the economy to improve is a bit like waiting for the weather to clear. You have no control over either. Boom and bust cycles have been the historical economic norm. The term "boom and bust" refers to the build-up in the price of a particular commodity or activity of a local economy. Bust is what happens when that build-up peaks and a downturn follows.

Boom and bust has existed for centuries, and despite optimistic predictions by politicians that boom and bust economics will be tamed, it's unlikely they will be. It is just a natural cycle of economic life. Some of the most famous booms have been the Californian Gold Rush, the roaring Twenties in the US followed by the Wall Street crash and the Great Depression. In recent years we've seen the burst of the 'dot.com bubble', where internet stocks soared to ridiculous prices based on nothing of any real value. And of course as I write this we are in the middle of one of the worst downturns in global history following an unprecedented boom.

Trying to get rid of boom and bust is impossible for the simple reason that it is a phenomenon caused by the fear and greed of individuals. As you can't eradicate human emotion—nor would you want to—the complete eradication of boom and bust cycles is impossible.

What people fail to understand, however, is that the very best time to make money is in a bust—not a boom! If the economy is booming you've missed the boat; the masses are already involved and are making uneducated choices about where to put their money based on financial advice that states they can't lose. The smart money has already pulled out because those who hold it can forecast the end of the cycle.

The idea, therefore, that you should wait until the economy is better in order to take your wealth creation seriously is fundamentally flawed. There will never be a better time to buy into property or to invest in a stock market portfolio. The market will recover, even from the financial crisis of 2008 onwards.

In the *Sunday Times Rich List 2009* the recession had wiped £155 billion from the fortunes of Britain's richest 1000 individuals—equivalent to one third of their wealth! The number of UK billionaires dropped from 75 to 43, but I don't imagine they will be *that* worried. These are smart men and women who know that the sun will rise again tomorrow and their fortunes will be regained with interest.

Few can believe that suffering, especially by others, is in vain. Anything that is disagreeable must surely have beneficial economic effects.

John Kenneth Galbraith

Empires built in times of recession

Let me ask you a question: what do Coors Beer, Wrigley's, IBM, UPS, General Motors, the Walt Disney Company, Hewlett-Packard, Toys-R-Us, Domino's Pizza and Microsoft have in common?

Apart from being extremely successful businesses, they were all started during an economic downturn.

Take Microsoft for example. When Bill Gates and Paul Allen got together, the US economy was in the doldrums and the country was still reeling from Watergate. Their first office was an Albuquerque motel room. The company worked away for a number of years making software using the BASIC programming language. Then in 1981, during another recession, Microsoft introduced MS-DOS, which catapulted it to the forefront of the industry. The rest is history.

The bottom line is, it doesn't matter what the economy is doing. Sure, it's easier to make money when things are going well but it's also easier to lose it if you don't know what you're doing. A poor economy demands passion, creativity and hard work in much the same way that a booming economy does!

Plus, if you are in business for yourself or are considering going into business then you are a lot more nimble than large organisations. You are therefore in a far better position to adapt to changing tastes and customer requirements.

Recessions and economic downturns are always amplified, not by straight economic conditions, but by people panicking. When talk of recession rears its ugly head, individuals worry about the future and tighten their purse. That impacts the circulation of money which in turn makes the economic situation worse, not better. The best way to deal with a recession is by positive action. Get better at your job or deliver greater value to your customers. Recession is a battle cry for improvement, not retreat.

Opportunities are everywhere. The recession might be drawing to a close, but its continuing legacy is employers' reliance on short-term staff. There may be fewer jobs for life, but there are more jobs in a lifetime.

Lucy Benington

Why this myth is so toxic

Like so many money myths this one places control for your own financial destiny outside of yourself and your own actions. But you can't control the economy, so if you sit around waiting for it to be perfect you'll never get off your backside and do anything.

The solution

Understand that there is no perfect economy. There is no perfect opportunity or perfect time—there is only right now!

So what if the pundits predict long-term gloom?! The world is still going to turn. People are still going to need products and services. If you have a dream or a plan, then research it. You have to match your offer to the market, but there is always room to make money in any economic climate. All you need is passion, commitment and a desire to succeed. Economic downturns offer an outstanding opportunity to create wealth because everyone else is retreating. Seize opportunities as they arise, and if they don't—make them.

New Rule of Wealth No. 8

Money will be made regardless of the economic climate.

You Need Luck To Become Wealthy

I've found that luck is quite predictable. If you want more luck, take more chances. Be more active. Show up more often.'

Brian Tracy

This myth comes in many forms, but the essence is always the same—luck, not planning or hard work—is the root cause of financial success. If you bought into the property market, you were lucky to have bought at the right time. If you invested in the stock market, you were lucky that your stocks performed well. It was, in effect, down to chance rather than good judgement.

Like the other myths, however, it's not true—at least it's not always true—which means that it is a meaningless statement. If there are exceptions to a rule, then there is no rule in the first place.

Money in mistakes

The classic business case study of the Post-It note is a great example of luck. Although of which type is open to opinion. When Spencer Sylver of 3M invented a weak adhesive that stuck to paper but could be removed without leaving a mark, there was no use for the invention—bad luck!

But necessity is the mother of invention, so when Arthur Fry was having problems at church with bookmarks that kept falling out of his hymnbook, he had an idea. As a colleague of Sylver he knew of the weak adhesive, so a sticky bookmark seemed like the perfect solution. You could argue that it was good luck that he was a chorister and made a connection.

But in reality it took ingenuity, determination and commitment to transfer that fluke invention into a money spinner that is still generating millions for 3M today.

_____

Luck. Take a second look at what appears to be someone's "good luck." You'll find not luck but preparation, planning and success-producing thinking.

David J Schwartz

Determination will always trump luck

If you consider the story of Rowland Hussey Macy you can't help but realise that luck, even bad luck, is usually irrelevant to success. His is probably not a name you are familiar with and yet he is the founder of the store in the US that bears his name—Macy's. His luck, as history would have it, was all bad and yet his name is a US institution. After at least five failed attempts to establish a retail store, he arrived in New York to try again. This time the store was robbed of $1000, and a few months after that a window fire caused $2000 damage. Considering his store was making $5 a day, these were both huge setbacks.

Macy would have been forgiven for throwing in the towel, but he didn't. He used his "bad luck" to propel him forward, and he went on to revolutionise retailing. Macy's was the first store to deal only in cash and use advertising to attract customers. Macy introduced the one-price system where the same item was sold to every customer for the same price—something we take for granted now! Many of his initiatives are now standard retailing practise, including clearance sales, free delivery and odd or fractional pricing to suggest a bargain. He also made business history by promoting a woman, Margaret Getchell, to an executive position.

The truth is, wealth is rarely an accident. More often than not it is the result of hard work and the right attitude. Luck—good or bad—is irrelevant. Intuition and persistence are important, and some of the most successful business people acknowledge that taking notice of gut instinct or intuition, and acting on it, has played a crucial role in their success.

Richard Branson's instincts and his willingness to follow them—often against the odds—have made him extremely wealthy. Branson says, following his decision to go into the airline business in 1984, "It was a move which in pure economic terms everybody thought was mad, including my closest friends, but it was something which I felt we could bring that others were not bringing." He followed his instincts and made his own "luck."

Wealth is a result of decisions made, actions taken and the attitude and expectation that you view things from. Your actions are directly shaped by your thoughts, feelings, beliefs and expectations around money, wealth and success. Those that make money at a serious level are no less or more lucky than everyone else. They are simply prepared so that when and if lady luck comes along, they are ready to take the fullest advantage.

The word "luck" is usually just a scapegoat for simply not trying, or laziness. Sure, luck sometimes plays a part in any success, but planning, enthusiasm and hard work are more likely to get you what and where you want than wishing your life away or waiting for the lottery to single you out. Sadly, there are thousands of people in this category. According to the July 2008 figures from the National Lottery, around 70% of UK adults play the lottery on a regular basis. Total annual sales of National Lottery products are greater than the combined annual sales of Coca Cola, Warburton Bread, Walkers Crisps, Hovis Bread, Cadbury Dairy Milk, Nescafé, Andrex, Lucozade, Kingsmill Bread and Robinson's Soft Drinks!

Lives come and go, hundreds of years of beating hearts have trusted in a bag of gold falling from the sky or waiting for some supernatural event that never arrived. What a waste! The Cavalry isn't coming.

The best luck of all is the luck you make for yourself.

Douglas MacArthur

Why this myth is so toxic

This myth, like so many others, is damaging because it puts your success outside of your control. If you believe that wealth is the result of fate or chance then you are waiting for lady luck to shine on you rather than making your own luck.

Instead of creating a plan and working that plan, people who believe this myth buy lottery tickets and waste what little money they do have hoping and praying that luck will make them rich.

The solution

Forget random luck—good or bad. You have to make your own luck through preparation, education and action. If you plan for the best, you will be ready to grasp opportunity when it shows up.

The simple truth is that when "luck" does turn up, it is rarely random—it happens to people who have worked hard and prepared for that moment.

New Rule of Wealth No. 9

Make your own luck—the Cavalry isn't coming.

If I Try To Be Wealthy and Lose It All, I Will Have Failed

Notice the difference between what happens when a man says to himself, I have failed three times, and what happens when he says, I am a failure.

S.I. Hayakawa

This myth leaves those who believe it in a permanent state of paralysis. Nothing will ever get done. On one hand the individual wants to achieve financial success and create wealth but they want to do so safely, with certainty and security. And that is simply not possible.

Failure itself is never the end of the line. Just look at Rowland Hussey Macy from the last chapter. He failed five times before he made a success of his business. If he had quit after he failed the first time, or the second or even the fifth, I wouldn't have been able to tell you in this book about the legacy he left to the world.

So what if you fail? Well, if you don't fail at some point, chances are you're not trying hard enough. It's impossible to be a success at anything without experiencing failure. Failure is a learning curve—an invitation to alter your actions and try a different approach. It's not a gravestone to be erected in respect of a "good effort." The only time you ever really fail is when you stop getting up and trying again.

Just as economies go through boom and bust cycles, there are many famous individuals who have done the same.

Failure should be our teacher, not our undertaker. Failure is delay, not defeat. It is a temporary detour, not a dead end. Failure is something we can avoid only by saying nothing, doing nothing, and being nothing.

Denis Waitley

Billions in the red

Take Donald Trump for example. Trump is actually an example of myth# 3—his father was a wealthy New York property developer, although his eventual fortune would go on to dwarf that of his father. His early success included the renovation of the Commodore Hotel into the Grant Hyatt, Trump Towers in New York and several other residential projects. His ambition culminated in business bankruptcy, with Trump himself on the brink of personal bankruptcy. Trump is reported to have said, "It's usually fun being The Donald, but in the early 1990s, trust me, it wasn't . . . I was many billions in the red." In his now famous moment of truth, he was walking down Manhattan's Fifth Avenue with Marla Maples when he spotted a beggar with a guide dog. He turned to Maples and said, "He's a beggar, but he's worth $900 million more than me today!" At the time he was in trouble to the tune of almost $1 billion on debt he had personally guaranteed. He had officially become very wealthy, and he had lost it all. But it didn't stop him.

"The Donald," as he refers to himself, isn't known for his lay-down-and-die approach to life. He fought back, and today he is worth an estimated $1.6 billion.

Edison's folly

Or what about Thomas Edison? We've all heard of his perseverence in creating the light bulb. The story goes that he tried some 10,000 times—way beyond what the average person would attempt. But did you know he also had some spectacular failures? He believed for example that iron could be extracted from low-grade ore, and his conviction cost him a great deal of money. At the time he was the world's foremost inventor. He had already invented the light bulb, the phonograph and umpteen other helpful products. Yet it didn't stop him losing a bundle on "Edison's Folly." But does history think any less of him because of it? No. History doesn't care. Chances are you never even knew about "Edison's Folly". All most people have heard about are the victories, the successes after repeated failure. Because that's all that really matters.

Ironically Edison once noted that genius is largely a matter of knowing what won't work!

Pouring good money after bad is never a smart idea. Repeating the same mistake over and over isn't smart either, but there are many people who have made rags to riches a round trip. These people are resourceful and ambitious and are able to build new wealth over and over again. Failure in one venture merely signals time for a change. So long as you learn from the errors, alter your plan and try again, then success is merely a matter of time.

Failure is not fatal, but failure to change might be.

John Wooden

Why this myth is so toxic

If you believe this myth, you just won't try. This symptom is seen in gifted athletes or musicians. They may have the raw talent but something—fear of failure?—holds them back from the total commitment to training and practice required to get to the top. Most success is more about perspiration than inspiration. It is the practice, the training, the unrelenting desire that transform talent into genuine skill and ability. Instead, believers in this myth aim low, console themselves with distant victories and the notion that they "could have been a contender."

The solution

If you don't try to create wealth, you won't create wealth. It's not rocket science. If you try and fail, then you have four choices:

- Give up and bore your friends to death about how you might have made it if it wasn't for X, Y or Z.
- Try again
- Try again, but tweak the plan
- Enlist somebody who is already successful

Often wisdom comes only through adversity—we have to fail our way to success.

Failure is not an end, just an opportunity for a new beginning. It doesn't mean you are a failure; it means your behaviour and actions didn't work, so change those, get up, dust yourself off and get back in the game. Self pity never made anyone rich.

New Rule of Wealth No. 10

Failure is often a prerequisite to success.

My Friends Would Resent Me If I Were Rich

Don't make friends who are comfortable to be with. Make friends who will force you to lever yourself up.

Thomas J Watson

If you believe this myth, my suggestion would be to get new friends! Friends who resent their friends' success aren't friends, and probably never were.

As human beings we work out what is acceptable behaviour and "normal" by watching those around us. This is how we learn, especially when we are very young. This means that parents, teachers, siblings, friends and close relatives exert a huge influence on what we believe about life and what to expect. Birds of a feather flock together, and there is safety in those numbers. The advantage of this type of learning is that it is fast, efficient and we gain a sense of belonging really quickly. The downside is that if for whatever reason you decide to step outside the unconscious boundaries that are created in this process, you will invariably meet with resistance.

Get the monkeys off your back

There is a famous experiment involving monkeys that illustrates very powerfully the potency of this need to conform. The monkeys were put into a large enclosure. Central to the enclosure was a tall wooden pole with a bunch of bananas on the top. As expected, the monkeys explored the enclosure and it wasn't long before they spotted the bananas. Only, whenever they tried to climb the pole to claim the bananas, they were blasted with a high-pressure water hose. The treatment didn't actually hurt the monkeys, but they got a fright and didn't particularly enjoy getting soaked. Eventually, after several attempts at the bananas which ended in them being soaked by the hose, they stopped trying to reach the bananas.

This wasn't too unusual and followed expected patterns. What was unexpected however was what happened when a new monkey was added to the group. One of the original monkeys was removed and replaced with a new monkey who had not experienced the water hose treatment. Although accepted by the group, as soon as he spotted the bananas and went to retrieve them, all the remaining monkeys pulled him off the pole—even though this time there was no water hose.

Soon even the new monkey stopped trying. Eventually all the monkeys who had personally experienced the water hose deterrent were replaced one by one and yet none of the new monkeys made any attempt at the bananas.

They had been conditioned to equate trying with pain, and it is this same conditioning that happens in families and friendships. Ironically, it is those closest to us that often discourage us the most from changing.

There are two reasons for this. The first is that they genuinely want to protect us from getting hurt, failing or feeling bad. Perhaps this is a throwback from their own failures which has been passed on by osmosis like the monkeys. The second reason, perhaps on a far more subconscious level, is that if you do change and you do take charge of your financial destiny and make more money, it will make them feel more inadequate for their own financial situation.

Birds of a feather flock together

Proverb

Friends and family are not always encouraging

As a result, you may be surprised to discover that your friends and family discourage you from changing. They will do everything in their power to "pull you off the pole." Partly because they don't want to see you fail and partly because they actually don't want to see you succeed either—otherwise they may have to change too.

You don't need to cut ties with all your family and friends. Just be very careful who you discuss your plans with. Don't broadcast your plans, just work away quietly without fanfare. Let your results speak from themselves.

If you notice that spending time with certain people depresses you or knocks you off course for a few days, then limit your time with them. People can only upset you if you allow them to.

If you hold yourself back from success in order to be accepted by your friends, nobody wins. You're letting them down, and worse, you're letting yourself down.

Besides, who says you have to shout about your success? In the book *The Millionaire Next Door,* authors Stanley and Danko discovered that there was a huge army of extremely wealthy families living quietly in the suburbs. Just because you create wealth and prosperity for yourself doesn't mean you have to drive a red Ferrari and live in Beverly Hills!

Jealousy is indeed a poor medium to secure love, but it is a secure medium to destroy one's self-respect. For jealous people, like dope-fiends, stoop to the lowest level and in the end inspire only disgust and loathing.

Emma Goldman

Why this myth is so toxic

This belief is not just toxic for you but for everyone in your social and business circle. If you accept mediocrity, it's likely others around you think that is acceptable too.

If you don't accept it, then you need to quit hiding behind people who do, and take a stand. If you want a better life, you need to make a better life. It's not going to fall in your lap.

The solution

Having like-minded people in your life is really important for happiness and personal fulfilment. There are few things more enjoyable than chatting to friends and enjoying good conversation. But it's unrealistic to think that all your friends will be interested in your endeavours to improve your financial affairs. It is possible, however, that some may also be interested in that outcome.

Finding people you can discuss your plans openly with is often a great benefit, and if you don't have those friends then perhaps you should consider creating what Napoleon Hill called "a mastermind group." Hill is of course famous for writing the first and perhaps best personal development book ever written—*Think and Grow Rich*. He talks of the importance of having a support system of those that can and want to help you in your quest. The mastermind, according to Hill, is the, "*coordination of knowledge and effort, in a spirit of harmony between two or more people for the attainment of a definite purpose.*"

So consider starting a select wealth creation club where you meet weekly to discuss your plans and what you have achieved—all committed to helping each other in any way possible to fulfil each person's chosen goals.

New Rule of Wealth No. 11

Your friends might find you a burden if you were poor!

I'll Save More Money When I Get More Money

Wealth can only be accumulated by the earnings of industry and the savings of frugality.

John Tyler

Yeah right, of course you will!

Millions of people, chock full of good intentions and little action, have said this to themselves for years. The sad truth is that for most people, the more they earn the more they spend.

It's known as golden handcuffs ... Once you are in a good job making loads of money, you won't save more money, you'll spend more money. The pressure to "keep up with the Joneses" will increase and every promotion will result in a desire to upgrade your life in some way to let everyone know that you're doing well.

The result is that you are chained to your job with golden handcuffs. They are golden because you make a very good wage, but they are still handcuffs because you are now bound to that job because you need the salary to service the debt you now find yourself in. The increase in salary hasn't given you more choice, but less, because you have let your spending match or even surpass your income, with disastrous consequences.

Delayed gratification

Delayed gratification, it would seem, is a thing of the past, and a decade of easy money has left us up to our necks in debt.

According to the Credit Action debt facts and figures compiled on 1st May 2009 the total personal debt for the UK to the end of March 2009 stood at

£1.459bn. Figures for the US are equally shocking. And it's not just individuals who have taken lending to a whole new level. The UK Government debt stands at £734.6bn which means that interest payments alone amount to a frightening £84m a day! This is projected to rise to £118m a day in the 2010/11 financial year.

As for savings, the statistics are very sorry indeed. Despite a decade where the economy was booming, almost a third (32%) of the British population does not have money set aside to help them cope if an emergency were to arise. The average amount each person believes they would need to cope in an emergency is £5,368.70—the approximate equivalent of four months' of the average person's take-home income, according to a 2009 NS&I (National Savings and Investments) Savings Survey.

Almost a quarter of people (24%) say they didn't have savings two years ago, and they still don't. More than a third of people (36%) say they have less money in savings now than two years ago, according to a poll conducted in March 2009 by moneysupermarket.com.

Nearly a third of adults would face financial disaster within two months if they lost their jobs, according to research for MoneyExpert.com. Half of them (15%) believe they would only last a month.

Clearly it doesn't matter how much people make, and assuming that we will save more when we make more is absolute rubbish.

Resolve not to be poor: whatever you have, spend less. Poverty is a great enemy to human happiness; it certainly destroys liberty, and it makes some virtues impracticable, and others extremely difficult.

Samuel Johnson

Make saving easy

As many as 14 million people say they cannot afford to set aside money for savings. However, a financial experiment conducted by AXA reveals that in just three months, people can train themselves to save without substantially affecting their lifestyle. Conducted in Britain, the research indicates that people treat money left in their current account after bills have been paid as the amount they need to live on and set their standard of living accordingly. If money is paid into a savings account on pay day the research demonstrates that they change their spending patterns and establish a new standard of living based on their remaining disposable income.

It is possible to save—you just have to make the effort and take the money out of your everyday bank account so that you never see it.

I've said it before, but creating wealth is not just about how much money you make, it's about how much you keep. Unless you make the sacrifice now, more money is unlikely to follow. And even if it does, if you don't get into the habit of saving, you'll just spend it when you get it anyway.

The only people getting rich from your excess are shop keepers and credit card companies.

In 2003, Barclays' then chief executive Matt Barrett gave evidence at the Commons' Treasury select committee investigating credit card charges and said, "I do not borrow on credit cards. It is too expensive. I have four young children. I give them advice not to pile up debts on their credit cards."

Convincing you that you don't need savings and you can rely on the never-never is big business, but if you are serious about creating long-term wealth, then you need to wake up and smell the coffee. You need to get into the habit of saving right now—not some mythical time in the future that will never come.

Granted, at the time of writing this, saving isn't very attractive with interest rates at a 315-year low! but saving is not just about the money. It's about developing the discipline of living within your means, of positive change, and of seeing yourself make progress. . . . and save. And while saving may not be attractive now, things will recover again—and you need to be ready to capitalise when they do.

Why this myth is so toxic

It lulls you into a false sense of security. You believe that one day you will get around to saving or making plans for your financial future, only you never do.

No one plans to retire with nothing. No one dreams of penny-pinching in their old age. Instead we hang on to an illusion that something will happen that will make it all work out. Some magic bullet will appear just at the last minute and save us from destitution.

Sorry to break the news to you, but that fairytale solution doesn't exist. There will be no fairy godmother to whisk you away to better things and turn your rags into robes.

Research by Key Retirement Solutions found that one in three pensioners still have an outstanding mortgage with an average mortgage debt of £43,069 and average monthly mortgage payment of £205. Do you think these people planned to still be in debt when they retired?

A *Daily Telegraph* survey found that almost one in ten adults belong to the "sandwich generation," where they have to help their children *and* their parents survive financially. Do you think anyone planned for that?

The only true failure lies in failure to start.

Harold Blake Walker

The solution

Next time you think about buying a new outfit or a new gadget—don't. If you have more than one credit card, do yourself a favour and cut them up.

If you want to be wealthy, you have to learn about delayed gratification. If you are smart with your money now you can create wealth that will look after you forever and allow you to indulge yourself. But if you indulge yourself now before you create the wealth, you will be running to a standstill your whole life.

By cutting back, by making sacrifices for the long-term, you'll be well on your way to clearing any debts you may have, building both discipline and character, and feeling more in control as you learn to live within your income. You need to learn to save more to have more, to multiply what you have through investment in your own financial future. When you have more, you will be able to give more and enjoy the life you deserve.

New Rule of Wealth No. 12
SAVE today or starve tomorrow.

You Have To Be Ruthless and Dishonest To Be Wealthy

He that is of the opinion that money will do everything may well be suspected of doing everything for money.

Benjamin Franklin

This myth probably has its roots in the notion that you have to be ruthless to be successful in business. For some reason there is a perception in business that the only way to succeed is to step over other people and that the good guys never finish first.

The media is often quick to point out how ruthless businessmen are and how they would sell their soul to the devil for profit. Bill Gates and Steve Jobs are high-profile men who have been branded ruthless on many occasions. But what exactly do we mean by the word "ruthless"?

Ruthlessness and dishonesty do not necessarily go together. Being dishonest to further your wealth creation activities is very different from being ruthless. Ruthlessness is a willingness to do what needs to be done and a single-minded determination. It doesn't mean dishonest and should not be construed as such.

This myth is also a similar idea to myth #1 which states that money is the root of all evil. But money itself is just a means of exchange—it acts as a mirror and illuminates people's true colours. If someone is corruptible and has flexible values and ethics, depending on the situation, money will exacerbate that and make it look as though they have been corrupted by the money itself. But the truth is—they were corrupted long before they had money.

Having a lot of money or having very little money doesn't relate to the type of person you are.

Of course there are examples where money has corrupted. There are examples where individuals have become ruthless *and* dishonest in order to perpetuate a lie and maintain an illusion of success. You just have to look back at the high profile corporate collapses of the last decade for proof.

The universal regard for money is the one hopeful fact in our civilization. Money is the most important thing in the world. It represents health, strength, honour, generosity and beauty. Not the least of its virtues is that it destroys base people as certainly as it fortifies and dignifies noble people.

George Bernard Shaw

No boundaries

Dennis Kozlowski, CEO of Tyco International was convicted of misappropriating more than $400 million of the company's funds, including $150 million in unauthorised bonuses to support a lavish lifestyle. His spending of corporate money was legendary. Tyco paid for his $30 million New York City apartment which included $6,000 shower curtains. The company also paid $1 million toward his second wife's 40th birthday party. Ironic for a man whose media rhetoric emphasized the importance of high ethical standards!

Kenneth Lay, Andrew Fastow and Jeff Skilling of Enron fame are also towering examples of how money and power can corrupt individuals. Kenneth Lay presided over some of the most creative accounting in corporate history and was quite happy to push Enron stock to workers while privately selling off huge chunks of his own shareholdings. CEO Jeffery Skilling and CFO Andrew Fastow were often described as "intimidating" and used to getting their own way. They refused to listen to anyone who raised questions about their practices and would make life very uncomfortable for those who did.

It's relatively simple to find evidence that this myth is correct but just because money corrupts some, it doesn't mean that it will or can corrupt everyone who succeeds in creating wealth—even vast wealth.

But not everyone

There are far more examples where vast fortunes have inspired great acts of philanthropy. We've already explored some of the most famous ones. For many people, money has been a blessing that can nurture and enhance all that is worthwhile in life.

As usual, it's not what or how much we have, but what we do with it that speaks volumes about who we are as people. If your intentions and actions are dishonest, then it's not so much that money has corrupted you, as much as you have corrupted money. Money is neutral. Use it for good and it can make wonderful things happen. Use it destructively and it will destroy you. Simple as that! It cannot corrupt you without your permission!

Why this myth is so toxic

If you believe that money is going to automatically turn you into a "bad" person, and you are not a bad person, then this myth is going to hold you back.

Making money a priority in your life means that you will need to change your behaviour and make new, better choices. It's going to require you to change your opinions and change how you spend your time. As Ghandi once said, "For things to change, I must change." If you want more money in your life, you are going to have to be willing to change the way you operate. If you think those changes will corrupt you and turn you into some money-grabbing monster then it's unlikely acquiring more money will have your true commitment.

The solution

Understand that money has no character of its own. All it does is bring out the person that you already are. What are your values? Get very clear about what you stand for and what you are willing to do to achieve your dreams and what you will not do. Create a personal code of conduct before you begin your wealth creation activity so that you can refer back to it when you need to.

This may sound like a silly idea but when Akito Morita and Masaru Ibuka started Sony after WWII the first thing they did was write down the company's philosophy. This simple act has since been rated as a pivotal and brave decision by Jim Collins in his classic business book *Built to Last*. Although the company's initial products did not survive, the company philosophy did and it kept Sony on its true path.

New Rule of Wealth No. 13

Money is neutral: the values of the individual will determine how it's managed.

14

It's Better to Give Than to Receive

Charity literally means love, the love that understands, that does not merely share the wealth of the giver, but in true sympathy and wisdom helps men to help themselves.

Franklin D Roosevelt

This myth is born out of religion. According to the King James Bible, Acts 20:35, "I have shewed you all things, how that so labouring ye ought to support the weak, and to remember the words of the Lord Jesus, how he said, It is more blessed to give than to receive." Like so many of the biblical phrases that work their way into every-day life, this one has been taken out of context. Perhaps the most important part is the first part of the sentence which refers to how we are given the capacity to work hard, and in doing so, we are given the opportunity to help others. It is the hard work or labouring which is so often missed in this quotation.

Whether you are religious or not, there are certain codes of conduct that most of us recognise as being right and wrong. If you ask most people whether it is right to steal, for example, they will say, "No." Whether or not we are consciously aware of these codes of conduct, there are certain things our society agrees as normal and acceptable, and other things that it does not.

You can't give what you haven't got or experienced

The idea that it is better to give than to receive is a religious adjunct to these social rules. We are led to believe that there is something more honourable in giving than in receiving. Yet how can we give if we have not first received?

This goes for money, love, compassion, trust or anything else you can think of. It's impossible for us to give love to another if we have not first received love from someone else. If we were not first loved by a parent or care giver, we wouldn't know what love looked like and therefore would be unable to pass it along to others.

We can't be kind to others unless someone has been kind to us first because we wouldn't understand what kindness was. So to say that it is better to give than to receive may be a nice, pious concept, but it's actually impossible.

How can we give money and support to others if we haven't first experienced how to make that money and be supported, whether from our family or from our own experiences? Being able to support yourself and create real wealth gives you opportunities to help others that go way beyond the odd donation in a bucket on the street.

Being able to give your time and energy can often be much more important than money alone. If you were in a better position financially, is it not true that you could be more available to your partner and your children? Would having more financial freedom not allow you to spend quality time with people you love, to help and support them through their formative years instead of working 18-hour days and forgetting their names?

If you were in a better financial position, you may find yourself in a better emotional position to give things to others that are far more valuable than money. You could give your time and your attention.

Giving is a good thing, something I enjoy quite a bit, but there's nothing wrong with receiving either. To say that one is better than the other is simply creating an unbalanced perspective. If you're uncomfortable about receiving things, you'll find ways not to—whether it's gifts, income—even compliments!

If my hands are fully occupied in holding on to something, I can neither give nor receive.

Dorothy Solle

Compliment others

What do you do when someone gives you a compliment? This simple test will show you whether you have a problem receiving. If you can't accept a compliment graciously and feel genuine pride in what someone says about you, then how will you be able to change your financial situation to create more wealth? If you can't accept a compliment, how do you think you'll cope with an increased bank balance?

As you become more successful, you must receive, otherwise why are you trying to make more money? To give a generous proportion to charity, education, leisure or your kids can all make you feel good, but money must first be received before you can give it away. To receive fair payment and profit for honest work is never something to feel ashamed about. It's called growth, and it's a natural part of our time on this planet.

Why this myth is so toxic

This myth implies some pious superiority for "giving" and at the same time implies that receiving is for the selfish. Those that truly believe this myth, perhaps because of religious teachings, are made to feel ashamed for feeling comfortable with receiving, and even for wanting to better themselves in economic terms.

Of course it is great to share your good fortune and to help people that you love and care for, but you have to help yourself first. This is not being selfish, it's common sense.

When the oxygen masks drop from the ceiling in an aircraft, the message is very clear—put your own mask on BEFORE you help others with their mask. This is not selfish, it's sensible. You are no use to your children or an ailing relative if in your frenzy to get their mask on, you pass out! All that means is that you make both of you vulnerable. If you help yourself first, you are then in the best position possible to help someone else.

The solution

Giving before you've received is impossible—you can't give something you don't have or have experience of. The only way to be able to give is to receive first. You need to make your financial well-being a priority so that you are in a position where you can give your money, time and energy to the people and causes you are passionate about.

God has given us two hands, one to receive with and the other to give with.

Billy Graham

New Rule of Wealth No. 14

To give, you must first receive. You can't impart what you don't have.

Money Doesn't Grow On Trees

Money is not given, it has to be raised. Money is not offered, it has to be asked for.

Aldous Huxley

Well, OK, this is a fact rather than a myth. (And although it's useful, I think it can be improved on!) Most children hear it at some time from their parents following persistent requests for money. Children initially don't appreciate the true value of money and are happy to spend it on meaningless rubbish that will be interesting for ten minutes and then forgotten.

It's every parent's role therefore to teach their children that money needs to be worked for, and this is the phrase that is invariably used to tell kids that it isn't that readily available.

It is an important lesson, and one that we all have to learn sooner or later. Money isn't infinite and it doesn't materialise out of thin air just because you want a new pair of shoes or couldn't possibly go out without a new outfit. It has to be earned first.

At least that's the way it used to work.

Your flexible friend

That is, until the advent of the credit card. John Biggins, an innovative banker at the Flatbush National Bank, New York, is responsible for your flexible friend. In 1947, he created a local community credit plan called "Charg-It" which covered a two-square-block patch around the bank.

The success of Biggins' idea attracted interest from other quarters. Two years later, Diners Club successfully launched their version of the credit card. Within a year of inception, Diners Club had managed to sign up 285 establishments and 35,000 cardholders—each paying $3 per year for the privilege.

Today the credit card business is booming. It reaps huge profits for the companies involved and causes plenty of sleepless nights for millions of overextended users. In less than 70 years there has been an explosion in credit cards allowing people easy access to money that people have not earned, and in many cases have no way of ever paying back.

According to Credit Action figures for May 2009, 20.3 million plastic card purchase transactions will be made today with a total value of £1.02bn. Total credit card debt in March 2009 was £53 bn. The UK collective credit limit on credit cards is £158bn, which is an average credit card limit of £5,129 per person. And best of all for the credit card companies is that the average interest rate on credit card lending is currently 17.6%, which at the time of writing was 17.1% above Bank of England base rate (0.5%).

The British Bankers' Association (BBA) reported that the number of credit card balances bearing interest in February 2009 was 73.4%. This means almost three quarters of all credit card users don't pay off their balance each month—although this is the *only* sensible way to use credit cards.

The idea that we can only buy what we can afford—that money doesn't grow on trees—has been lost in a frenzy of easy money.

And as we'll see in myth #20—debt is the death knell to any aspirations you have of financial freedom—certainly credit card debt!

The key to money is that it is a means of exchange. You are supposed to get money in return for something else. You go to work and do your job, and in return you are paid. You invest your money into property, and in return you are rewarded with more money. Access to money without effort is a fast track to disaster.

We all know that money doesn't grow on trees, but we behave as though it does. We feel we deserve to get rich without effort or persistence. We don't want to wait while the tree grows from a seed. We expect a fully formed, fruit-bearing tree in our back garden the minute we plant it. Nature doesn't work like that, however, and neither does money.

Work hard. Hard work is the best investment a man can make.

Charles M Schwab

How to make money grow

There is a similarity between money and a tree, however. Both need to be planted somewhere that will allow the seed to grow. Both need to be nurtured and cared for. For money, we need to save some, and this acts as the seeds to wealth. Once we have the seeds, we need to invest those seeds wisely in fertile soil so they can grow into a powerful fruit-bearing tree. If we do that, our money will provide years of enjoyment, sustenance and shelter, as well as providing seeds to create even more money trees.

But this takes time. You can't seriously expect your money tree to magically appear overnight like Jack's beanstalk. That may happen in fairytales, but it doesn't happen in real life, and the sooner you accept that and get on with the job of creating real wealth, the better.

Besides, if money did grow on trees, we wouldn't value it—that's why the global economy is in such a pickle. Money is best enjoyed when honestly made and freely given—like love. When we spend money we didn't earn, it is meaningless, and we feel little responsibility to pay it back. This is evidenced by the fact that in the UK alone, 323 people will be declared insolvent or bankrupt today according to Credit Action. R3, the association of business recovery professionals, estimates this will increase to 435 people per day throughout 2009, or one person becoming bankrupt or entering into an Individual Voluntary Arrangement (IVA) every 3.3 minutes.

We have to take responsibility for money and truly appreciate its value if we are ever to harness its awesome power. We have a duty of care to teach those principles to our children so they will not find themselves saddled with debt as they enter their adult life. Spoiling our children is counter-productive to their long-term wealth and happiness.

If you cannot make money on one dollar, if you do not coax one dollar to work hard for you, you won't know how to make money out of one hundred thousand dollars.

E.S. Kinnear

Why this myth is so toxic

In truth, this saying isn't really damaging. (And obviously, it isn't a myth either!) In fact, if you remember it, you may have a healthy respect for money rather than assuming it's "easy come, easy go," Having said that, it may limit your thoughts and produce the feeling that making money is always a flat-out struggle against the odds, in which case you won't take the actions necessary to plant your money trees.

You have to balance a respect for money with an understanding that you have to do something and add value to really make money.

The solution

Money doesn't grow on trees—that's obvious—but it grows like trees. The accumulation of money is very similar to the creation of an orchard. You have to plant the seeds, feed and nurture those tender early shoots and resist the temptation to eat the early fruit. You have to take a longer-term view in order to reap the true rewards.

New Rule of Wealth No. 15

Money grows LIKE trees.

Myth

16

Do What You Love And The Money Will Follow

What we really want to do is what we are really meant to do. When we do what we are meant to do, money comes to us, doors open for us, we feel useful, and the work we do feels like part of us.

Julia Cameron

This myth is a consequence of the new age personal development movement which encourages people to pursue their dreams.

Ever since Napoleon Hill wrote *Think and Grow Rich,* an industry has grown up around the ideas that were contained in it. Hill was essentially commissioned by Andrew Carnegie to research the wealthiest and most successful men of the time to uncover if there were any common denominators or hallmarks for greatness that could be taught to others. Carnegie invited Hill to dedicate his life to that quest and gave him unparalleled access to people like Henry Ford, Theodore Roosevelt, Charles Schwab, John D. Rockefeller, Thomas Edison and F.W. Woolworth. Obviously, Hill jumped at the chance, and as a result, he is considered by many as the father of personal development.

Since then we have all been encouraged through seminars, books and DVD programmes to follow our heart, find out what we enjoy doing and make a living out of that. The mantra is—do what you love and the money will follow.

But what if doing what you love is growing vegetables in your back garden or crocheting table cloths? Realistically, these things are not going to necessarily make you money, let alone make you rich.

This idea needs therefore to be tempered with reality and business acumen. If you have discovered a way to make your vegetables particularly tasty or grow particularly fast, then perhaps you have the seed of an idea that can be built upon, otherwise it's never likely to be your pot of gold at the end of the rainbow.

Don't cut off your nose to spite your face

I see many people in my seminars who are desperate to make more money. Some are making a good living or already have a thriving business, but they can't make the transition into serious wealth. More often than not, my seminars on wealth creation are not the first they have attended, and many have already come across this myth. They feel somehow ashamed of the fact that they don't enjoy their business or don't rush to work in the morning bursting with enthusiasm.

I've spoken to business owners who are seriously considering quitting the business or selling it so they can pursue something they genuinely love, even though they have no idea what that might be.

Why on earth would you want to throw away the vehicle that could make you wealthy beyond your dreams because of a misguided idea that you should be loving every minute of your business life.

Sure, having an interest in what you do certainly helps and should be aspired to, but there are a number of major challenges with this myth.

We are at our very best, and we are happiest, when we are fully engaged in work we enjoy on the journey toward the goal we've established for ourselves. It gives meaning to our time off and comfort to our sleep. It makes everything else in life so wonderful, so worthwhile.

Earl Nightingale

Uncovering natural talent

For a start, most people haven't got a clue what they love to do. They are so busy making a living they have no time to build a life. Most people fall into their professions by accident—their job or business is therefore a means to an end rather than a vocation. But there is nothing wrong with that. This myth makes it sound as though there is.

Most people stumble into something they are interested in or passionate about, and when they do they should be encouraged to pursue that interest, maybe find ways to make a living from it and even create real wealth from it. But if that doesn't happen, you can still create wealth.

The second thing that is wrong with this myth is that it pulls someone's focus away from their job or business. You will never make more money at your job if you do it half-heartedly. You will never get that promotion, and you'll therefore never be in a position to use that extra money to create long-term wealth. If you already have a business, it will never become a money-making machine if you are constantly looking over your shoulder for something better. If the business already works, then put your focus on that so it frees up your time to explore other options. A good business will not need you in it to make money, and that should give you the freedom to find the niche you will love.

And when you do, you won't be stressed out trying to turn it into a money-making venture; you can just enjoy it for what it is.

There can be no doubt that loving what you do helps you make money. I'm not disputing that. What I am disputing is that you have to love what you do in order to make money—or that loving something is a fast track to automatic wealth.

Nassim Nicholas Taleb is not a name you may be familiar with, but he is the former "quant" analyst and derivatives trader who made $40 million from shorting the market on Black Monday in 1987. Taleb has since written several brilliant books on randomness and is currently the Dean's Professor in the Sciences of Uncertainty at the University of Massachusetts. Did he love what he did? No, his writing is filled with contempt for his profession, and he believes that most city traders are like children picking pennies off the road in front of a steamroller. He believes that the majority of those inside the money markets have no idea what they are doing or the potential damage they can cause—a theory that has largely been borne out by the global financial difficulties we have seen in the past.

But regardless of how he felt about it, it offered him an opportunity to pursue what he is interested in, and he is now described as one of the most sought after thinkers in the world today.

Why this myth is so toxic

This myth is damaging because it's not always true. The fact is, most of us haven't a clue what we are especially good at. We have no idea what our natural talents are, or even if we have any, so this myth makes us feel especially inadequate! We get to feel bad twice—about not knowing what we love AND about not making enough money.

Knowing what interests you can certainly help you succeed because you will lose track of time, and work will not seem like work. But until you find it, use what you have and are right now. That's more than enough for you to create wealth with!

When you are not passionate about your work, chances are you're not as turned on about life as possible. People who know their purpose tend to have more energy, enthusiasm and joy at work and at home. You can identify your purpose by exploring your passions. Look at who you are passionate about "being" rather than just what you are passionate about "doing".

Marcia Wieder

The solution

Whether you have a job or run a business, do it to the best of your ability—decide to love it! Even if it's not your passion, find something you can love—the feeling of accomplishment in a job well done, or the pride in the relationships you develop. Enjoy helping others, and use the money you create from that role to invest in a better life for yourself.

If you really detest your job, then get off your backside and find something you will enjoy better. If you don't know what that is, think back on your life and try to work out what sort of roles you've enjoyed. Think also about the working environment you've most enjoyed and find a good match.

Complete some of the personality profiling techniques that are available. One that is particularly helpful in working out what you are naturally inclined toward is called the ID System. Others include Myers Briggs and the Disc profile.

Get to know yourself better and find ways to be more fulfilled in your work and home life. If those things can also make you money, then great!

New Rule of Wealth No. 16
Add value and the money will follow.

I'd Have To Work Even Harder To Get Rich; It's Just Not Worth It

Many people take no care of their money till they come nearly to the end of it, and others do just the same with their time.

Johann Wolfgang Von Goethe

This myth is borne out of the fact that most people are running to stand still when it comes to money. They are like ducks on a pond, calm above the water and paddling like crazy to stay afloat under the water.

This sad situation is usually a consequence of that easy money we've been talking about. When people buy what they can't really afford, they increase the amount of "must" money they need each month. This is the money they MUST make just to survive. When all your income is eaten up by "must" money and there is nothing left over, it's an extremely stressed way to live.

One of the solutions that people consider is to take a second job or to work longer hours, so by the time they get home after an 18-hour day, the idea of doing anything other than collapsing on the couch isn't very appealing.

But is this really any way to live?

Work harder, not smarter

This is a myth because it doesn't have to be true. If you resonate with this myth then chances are you need to work smarter not harder. There are only 24 hours in every day regardless of your wealth or financial situation, so you have to find ways to use those hours in a way that is going to help you out of the struggle you currently experience.

If you don't, then you will be collapsing on the couch for the next 40 years until finally you never get back up again and wonder what the hell it was all for.

The assumption is that you have to work like a dog to be wealthy. If you relate to this myth, you are already working like a dog (and maybe you're broke and miserable too!) so surely taking a step back and finding a smarter way of working is preferable to the ongoing prospect of stress and exhaustion.

I'm not saying a few weeks of change are suddenly going to lift you out of the mess. But I am saying that unless *you* decide to change something, *nothing* is going to change, and you will still be paddling like crazy in ten years time.

If I could show you a way to make those changes, take small incremental shifts to your behaviour that would guarantee that you have peace of mind in retirement, that you would be debt-free and create long-lasting wealth into the future in exchange for a little effort and a few changes up front, you would be mad not to take me up on it.

Creating your own wealth is always worth some sacrifice up-front.

Money is plentiful for those who understand the simple laws which govern its acquisition.

George S. Clason

Time is your most precious resource

Your most precious resource is not money, it's time. You can always make and spend more money, but you can never make more time. Once it's gone, it's gone. It is this simple fact that makes compound interest so powerful.

Did you know, for example, that if your grandparents invested £1000 into an investment account paying 9% when you were born, the rule of 72 states that it would take 8 years to double (72/9=8). Say that money was forgotten about and the interest compounded. By the time you were 48, that £1000 investment would be worth a staggering £64,000!

Time makes money too.

So what do you do with your time? No, really, what do you actually do with it? Are you really passed out on the couch or are you up for another five hours watching *Big Brother* or some other waste-of-space reality show? When you are online, are you doing something useful or important, or gossiping with your mates on MSN? Do you check your e-mails twenty times a day or spend half your life with a mobile phone squashed to your ear?

Perhaps it's time to get smart with how you spend your most precious resource so you can create the other precious resource—money.

Opportunity is missed by most because it is dressed in overalls and looks like work.

Thomas Edison

Why this myth is so toxic

It's damaging because it's not necessarily true, and believing it will stop you from changing your habits and behaviours to ones that will support your long-term financial well-being.

If you are already tired and run down and feel you are always struggling to get by, there is zero incentive to change if you believe in your heart that it's not possible because you don't have the time.

It's also a cop-out and I think we both know it!

The solution

Keep a time diary and make a note of what you do every day for a week. This will allow you to get clear about the facts, not fiction about how you spend your time.

If you discover that you actually have several hours a day where you could be doing something more productive, then you have the capacity to change your financial future.

You have to decide whether *Big Brother* or *Eastenders* is more important than creating wealth and securing your financial future.

Make a list of what you want to be and have and what isn't working. And resolve to do what needs to be done—regardless of how hard it may seem at the start.

New Rule of Wealth No. 17

You have to work SMARTER to be rich.

It Takes Money To Make Money

All riches have their origin in the mind. Wealth is in ideas—not money.

Robert Collier

There are elements of truth in this myth, but the implied assumption that you need lots of money to make money is most certainly not true.

It is possible to make money out of thin air by applying talent and ability. An artist can paint a masterpiece using materials that may cost a few pence, but sell it for considerably more. A writer can create value with pen and paper. But they still need money to buy the raw materials.

In business terms it is true that you need some money to create real wealth, but the main ingredient in success is determination, not money.

Take Mary Kay Ash for example. Her childhood was not easy; her father was incapacitated with tuberculosis, and the family relied on the wages of her mother who ran a restaurant. As the only child at home, and with a mother out working, Mary Kay had to cook, clean and do most of her own shopping. Her mother, aware of the burden she was under, used to leave her daughter messages that always ended with, "Honey, you can do it."

Mary Kay took the message to heart, and it was one she would rely on her whole life. Her family didn't have the money to send her to college. (See next myth!) She married a local radio personality, and by the time he was called to serve in WWII, they had three kids. She supported her family during his service, and they divorced shortly after his return, leaving her to raise three kids on her own.

She had no money, but she did have resilience and a determination to look after her family. Mary Kay became a direct sales representative for Stanley Home Products—frequently holding three home demonstrations a night. Obviously, she didn't subscribe to the previous myth.

She created Mary Kay Cosmetics in 1963 using what little life savings she had, and went on to create an empire. The company was built on the Golden

Rule: Treat others as you would like them to treat you. Clearly she also didn't believe in myth #13 either!

Money is the seed of money, and the first guinea is something more difficult to acquire than the second million.

Jean Jacques Rousseau

Do whatever it takes

Or what about Peter Jones' story? Perhaps best known for being on the panel of entrepreneurs of the UK version of the hit TV business investment show *Dragon's Den,* Peter Jones is a shining example of myth #10—he did lose it all and he did fail. It left him with no money at all. But it didn't stop him from becoming a very wealthy man.

His first venture was setting up a tennis academy at just 16. Then he moved into manufacturing computers, and in his mid-twenties he opened a cocktail bar. He lost money on the cocktail bar, and in his late twenties he lost the computer business too because customers didn't pay up. He was forced to give up his home and his sports cars and move back in with his parents. It couldn't have been an easy time!

But he never lost sight of his goal. And he was willing to do anything to achieve it—including swallowing his pride and getting a job! He joined Siemens Nixdorf and excelled, becoming the head of their PC business in the UK.

He was smart about what he did with his salary, and over the following few years made enough money to set up his next venture—Phones International Group—in 1998. Today he's worth an estimated £157m. Peter Jones never gave up and was willing to eat humble pie along the way. He didn't see his experiences as failures, just stepping stops to success, and he was willing to do whatever it took to get some working capital together to try again.

You can't make money out of thin air, so in that respect there is some validity in this myth—but you don't need thousands to get started.

The evidence unmistakably indicates that you have to spend money in order to make money.

Srully Blotnick

A little can go a long way

In truth, it takes surprisingly little money to start a small business from home. Think about how much you're spending on cigarettes, booze or club memberships. How far could more prudent spending take you? If you saved that wasted money and invested it wisely in starting a home business—even if it was just supplementing your salary at first—wouldn't that be more exciting and rewarding than wasting it on a hangover?

If you believe that it's lack of money stopping you, you're wrong. It's you! As my Dad used to say: *"It's what you do with what you have!"* There are many ways to make money, first in small ways you might not have considered. If it's pride that's holding you back from becoming wealthy, then stay poor! You might not start out doing the thing you want, but see the alternative pursuit as a stepping stone. It could just give you enough, perhaps on a part-time basis, to invest in your bigger dream.

Starting small can help you to learn the prudent use of money and how to manage the rollercoaster of emotions that wealth creation can create. You'll appreciate the value of sacrificing the small things now for the bigger things later once you have them.

It takes enthusiasm to make money. Passion, planning and knowledge are also essential—oodles of cash in the bank is not. And you need support and good people around you.

You also need to do work that makes you dog-tired at the end of the day, but which lifts you out of bed with a song the following morning because you can't wait to get started. All this and a little money can go a long way!

Why this myth is so toxic

If you genuinely believe that you need money to make money, and more specifically that you need a lot of money to make money, then you will never even try to accumulate that money, never mind using what you save or make to generate even more.

This myth makes you feel better about wasting the money you do have on dead-end pursuits.

I'm not saying that you have to live like a monk, but what do you actually spend your money on? Does it really add value to your life and make you happy, or just momentarily numb the unhappiness and lack of fulfilment you feel? Wouldn't you rather be excited about your life and what you can create?

The solution

How can you make more money right now? Is that just spending less, or do you have skills, interests, knowledge or abilities that could create a supplementary income?

We all have to start somewhere, and the first step is taking responsibility for your current financial situation. You don't need thousands in the bank to get creative with the money you already make, so save more and be creative with your time. Once you get into the way of saving and investing, the rest is easy. It's making the effort to create that first new pound that is often the hardest.

New Rule of Wealth No. 18

It takes enthusiasm, creativity and determination to make money.

I Have To Be Well-Educated To Become Wealthy

Formal education will make you a living; self-education will make you a fortune.

Jim Rohn

This myth is just plain wrong and has no redeeming features whatsoever.

If it were correct, then university professors, scientists and academics would be driving Ferraris and wearing Armani suits. Instead, they are more likely to drive a 15-year-old car and wear brown cords and a jacket with frayed cuffs.

Don't get me wrong. I have the utmost respect for highly-educated individuals, but to say that wealth is dependent on education is a fallacy.

There are, of course, some very well-educated individuals who make a serious amount of money. Doctors, lawyers and dentists, to name a few. But like highly-paid executives, their real wealth comes from what they do with their earnings rather than the earnings themselves. They end up rich because they invest their money wisely and grow it over the longer term.

But what about the truly wealthy? Many of the names that spring to mind have no degrees apart from the honorary ones that universities dish out when you are really wealthy!

Bill Gates was made an honorary Doctor of Law at Cambridge University in June 2009, along with his wife Melinda. Nine years previously the couple donated £100m to set up a scholarship programme to enable outstanding foreign graduates to study at Cambridge.

Part of the Microsoft legend is around the fact that Bill Gates actually dropped out of Harvard to pursue his business ambitions.

Education costs money, but then so does ignorance.

Sir Claus Moser

University drop-out to multi-millionaire

In December 1974, Paul Allen was on his way to meet his high school friend, Bill Gates, at his dorm room at Harvard. On route he bought a copy of *Popular Electronics*. The cover showed the Altair 8080 under the headline, "World's First Microcomputer Kit to Rival Commercial Models." Gates rang the makers of the Altair (MITS) and informed them that they had developed a BASIC programming language that could be used on the Altair. MITS were interested and wanted to see it. Only neither Allen nor Gates had written a single line of code; they didn't have an Altair or the chip that ran the computer.

But they found a way, and eight weeks later Allen flew to MITS to demonstrate the program, having never tested it on an Altair. The demonstration went perfectly and MITS arranged a deal with Gates and Allen to buy the rights to their BASIC. Within the year Gates had dropped out of Harvard, he and Allen created Microsoft, and a legend was born.

This sort of story is not a one-off. Far from it. Sergey Brin and Larry Page both dropped out of Stanford University to pursue Google, now Microsoft's biggest competitor!

Sergey Brin moved to the United States when he was six years old. He did an undergraduate degree at the University of Maryland and was obviously no intellectual slouch. He followed in his father's and grandfather's footsteps by studying mathematics, double-majoring in computer science. After graduation, he moved to Stanford to study for his PhD in computer science. This is where he met his intellectual soul mate, Larry Page, and they became close friends. In a crammed dorm room full of inexpensive computers, they built Google using data-mining systems. The program became popular in Stanford, and the pair suspended their PhD studies to start up Google in a rented garage. Today they are reportedly worth about $12 billion each.

Advertising legend David Ogilvy was kicked out of Oxford because he couldn't pass the exams. Michael Dell abandoned his studies at the University of Texas to concentrate on his direct selling computer business. Even John F Kennedy Jr. was rejected from Harvard and failed the New York bar exam twice, but it didn't stop him becoming one of America's most popular presidents.

In my early life, and probably even today, it is not sufficiently understood that a child's education should include at least a rudimentary grasp of religion, sex and money. Without a basic knowledge of these three primary facts in a normal human being's life—subjects which stir the emotions, create events and opportunities, and if they do not wholly decide, must greatly influence an individual's personality—no human being's education can have a safe foundation.

Phyllis Bottome

Just know who to ask

It's not about whether or not you are educated, it's about whether you are smart. You don't need to know all the answers—you just need to know where to go to get the answers. Andrew Carnegie knew nothing about the actual process of steel production, but he still created a formidable empire.

Henry Ford was considered ignorant by many of the intellectual snobs of his time because he wasn't "educated," yet he was smart enough to hire the brightest people and pay them to provide him with the information he needed.

Education of the academic kind is great for those who want it and need it. But there are other ways to express and develop intelligence which are not found in textbooks. Making money is as much about being street smart and intuitive as it is about formal education. Too much information can hold us back and keep us in a state of perpetual indecision. Sometimes you just have to trust your gut and make it happen.

Not everyone has the opportunity to go to university. That may be because of a lack of cash or a lack of application, but university is not a free pass to wealth. In fact, recent figures show that the average UK student graduate is £14,161 in debt! That sort of debt makes it very hard to create anything but more debt!

Being smart is essential for success and wealth, but being educated in academic institutions is nothing more than a personal choice.

Why this myth is so toxic

It's a form of intellectual snobbery that implies that the only way to be clever is by having letters after your name. And if you believe it, and you don't happen to have letters after your name, then you won't believe that wealth creation is for you.

But just because you don't have a university education, it doesn't mean you can't create wealth. This myth is nothing more than a justification for inactivity.

The solution

Forget the myths and have a look at real life. We have all met people who are super smart but who are rude, arrogant and broke with it.

Entrepreneurial spirit is not something you learn in a classroom, but something you experience in the real world. If you love learning, then continue to do so—turn your ferocious appetite for knowledge onto wealth creation and make a real difference to your future.

New Rule of Wealth No. 19

Be smart with your time and resources to be wealthy.

I Have Too Much Debt

Avoid borrowing money to display the appearances of wealth—the eyes of others will destroy you.

Ben Benson

This may seem like a statement of the obvious rather than a myth. But the problem is, it doesn't differentiate between good debt and bad debt.

Good debt Vs bad debt

Good debt is debt that makes you money. So if you borrow money to invest in a buy-to-let property where the rent exceeds the mortgage and expenses, then that is good debt. If you borrow money to invest in a business which creates money, then that is good debt. Basically, it is any borrowing that is used to increase your wealth.

Everything else is bad debt. That means your personal loans, all your credit cards, hire purchases or overdrafts.

According to the May 2009 Credit Action fact sheet, the total UK personal debt at the end of March 2009 stood at £1,459bn. The average household debt in the UK is £9,280 (excluding mortgages). This figure increases to £21,580 if the average is based on the number of households who actually have some form of unsecured loan. The interest repayments on personal debt in Britain were £69bn in the last 12months. The average interest paid by each household on their total debt is approximately £2,760 per annum.

During March 2009, Britain's personal debt increased by £1m every 50 minutes. And if you think that is bad, consider how much it's reduced as a result of the credit crunch. In January 2008, Britain's personal debt increased by £1m every 5.3 minutes. No, that is not a typo—£1m every 5.3 minutes!

The only wealth that bad debt creates is for the companies supplying it. I'm sorry to be the bearer of bad news, but the simple truth is that having too much bad debt *does* prevent you from creating real wealth. It is not a myth!

Man was lost if he went to a usurer, for the interest ran faster than a tiger upon him.

Pearl S Buck

Your mortgage is bad debt too

And it gets worse—you know that home you were told was going to be an asset? It's bad debt too. Your home does not make you money? Not unless you rent out rooms to students or sell it—but then where will you live?—So in the strictest sense of the word, your home is not an asset, it's a liability.

We have been told for generations that renting is dead money, and property booms encouraged us to buy instead of rent, but all that is changing again. The only reason it's better to buy than rent is that sometimes it is possible to pay a mortgage that is less than or similar to the rent in that area. Then it makes sense.

The smart people are the ones who worked this out before the property booms and who consequently became wealthy—especially as the asset increased in value and more and more people jumped on the property-investing bandwagon. Don't get me wrong, there is still money to be made in property, but like everything else, you need to know what you are doing. You need to be smart.

As for the banks, they have come up with new and novel ways for you to increase your debt. It's called a "home equity loan" and it has allowed people to access money they didn't know they had, and it extended the life of their mortgage well into their retirement years to boot.

A home equity loan might sound like a good idea, and if you use it to invest in profit-generating investments, it can be a great vehicle for wealth creation, but if you draw down that money to buy a surround-sound home entertainment unit or go on a six-month cruise or buy a new car, then you are, financially speaking at least, an idiot!

I don't mean to be rude, but these are the cold, hard facts. Remember the statistics from myth #12. One in three pensioners still has an outstanding mortgage with an average mortgage debt of £43,069 and average monthly mortgage payments of £205. As more and more people cash in the equity in their homes, this phenomenon is set to continue. Far from being debt-free and cashed-up in retirement, people are going to be stressed out and living in one room because they can't afford heating *and* their mortgage repayments! Is that really the way you want to spend the twilight years of your life?

Or do you want to get smart about your financial future NOW so you can go on cruises then and enjoy all the very best the world has to offer without worrying about money or Monday mornings?

Most people have debt. But we have forgotten the distinction between good debt and bad debt. Instead, we have created a society of buy now, pay later—where banks, certainly a few years ago, were throwing money at anyone with a pulse. It is that attitude that has landed the developed world in financial hot water.

Why this myth is so toxic

This myth is damaging because it is financially illiterate. Bad debt is extremely damaging to your wealth-creation plans. I would go so far as to say that if you have large debts on credit cards or personal loans, then it's impossible for you to create wealth. The interest you are paying on those loans is huge—many, many times more than you could ever make on even the most speculative investments.

Where do you know that you could invest your money and get a 17.6% return on it? Yet that's the average interest rate on UK credit cards. In 2004, the Competition Commission investigated door-to-door lending following a complaint from the National Consumer Council. Door-step lending is big business in the poorer areas of the UK—worth an estimated £2bn. The NCC found that the average interest rates were 177% with some instances in excess of 1000%. Do you know anywhere that you can receive those sorts of returns? No, it's impossible.

And so it's impossible to create wealth when you have bad debt—you are always behind the eight ball.

The myth that is doing the real damage to us individually and as a society is that debt is good, or even necessary, if we want the lifestyle we aspire to. If used properly to buy things that make money, debt can be good, but for everything else, it's a dream killer.

I've got all the money I'll ever need, if I die by four o'clock.

Henny Youngman

The solution

To move forward, you might need to sell some of what you have. Whatever you do, you must pay off your bad debts and make some smarter choices.

There is always a solution, and if you just put your ego aside and think of your long-term happiness and security, you might be willing to downsize your family lifestyle to create real wealth. One thing is for sure, you will continue to dig a deeper and deeper hole for yourself if you don't clear your debt.

Do you really need that second car? Do you really need the first one? Does it need to be so big? Do you need the new plasma-screen TV? Is High Definition really worth the contribution it makes to a lifetime of financial misery? Will you really be happier because of a house extension? Is it really necessary to have a five-star holiday abroad?—Isn't it true you'd probably have just as much fun somewhere cheaper?

There used to be a time when, if people couldn't afford something, they did without or saved up until they could buy it outright.

What's changed? We think debt is OK! It's not. It's a slow ligature, and a nation chokes while whole economies sell their souls to it.

It's amazing what you can do without. We set our desires on wants when all we need are needs. As the wise Thorstein Veblen told us so long ago, "superfluous wealth buys only superfluities."

We have superfluous debt—billions of it, and it's making us very sick.

Bad debt diminishes the human spirit, warps our desires and crushes our soul. It's not normal to lie awake at night worrying about money—especially money we have spent that we never actually had! It's no way to live. Learn to say "No" to your kids and mean it. You are doing them no favours otherwise. And while you're at it, learn to say "No" to yourself too, until you really can afford to live the way you want to.

New Rule of Wealth No. 20

Investment debt is a requirement to building wealth; consumer debt should be avoided like the plague.

I Don't Deserve To Be Rich

If you don't change your beliefs, your life will be like this forever. Is that good news?

Dr Robert Anthony

Hey, look, maybe you don't! Maybe you would rather lie on the couch and watch *Big Brother* after all, buying your lottery tickets week in, week out, hoping that some day your ship will come in.

It might. But it's extremely unlikely—sort of 1 in 14,000,000 unlikely. But if you like those odds, knock yourself out!

What the myth that you don't deserve to be rich is really all about is your beliefs.

As we grow up, we work out what is acceptable and normal by looking around us and seeing what people around us are doing. What we are told, therefore, in the formative years of our life can have a profound effect on what we believe to be true, and perhaps more importantly, what we believe to be possible.

Competing forces

We have two minds—the conscious mind and the subconscious mind. Everything that ever happens to you is stored in the subconscious mind, every conversation, every thought. There is even evidence that the subconscious mind knows things that the conscious mind has forgotten or never even knew. Bruce Lipton in his book *The Biology of Belief: Unleashing the Power of Consciousness, Matter & Miracles* calls the subconscious mind "a repository of stimulus-response tapes derived from instincts and learned experiences. The subconscious mind is strictly habitual; it will play the same behavioural responses to life's signals over and over again, much to our chagrin."

We have all experienced the subconscious in action when a friend or colleague has said something, and we've flown into a rage or sulked for twenty minutes, and later wondered why we got so emotional. "You" didn't get emotional—something in the environment triggers a past memory or response, and your subconscious mind delivers the "appropriate response." It's like the doctor tapping your knee with that little hammer and your leg flying up—you didn't make that happen, but it happened nonetheless.

The subconscious is therefore incredibly powerful, and it stores all sorts of information that will 'help' you navigate life. Only, some of it isn't accurate. It doesn't differentiate between opinion and fact. So if you were told things enough in your early life, you will begin to believe them, and those thoughts and beliefs will become your jailor.

In India, they train baby elephants by tying their leg to a tree when they are very small. Of course the baby elephant pulls and yanks his hardest and doesn't manage to escape. After a while he stops pulling, and so when he's an adult, the owner only has to put a rope on the elephant's leg and it will stay where it's put. The elephant doesn't realise that he is no longer attached to the tree or that even if he was, he is now so powerful and strong he could rip the tree up by its roots.

Your beliefs act in much the same way.

Your subconscious mind is considerably more powerful than your conscious mind, and if you consciously want to create money in your life, but subconsciously don't believe you deserve money because of a plethora of distant reasons, then I'm afraid to say the subconscious will win.

As Lipton puts it: "If the desires of the conscious mind conflict with the programs in the subconscious mind, which 'mind' do you think will win out? You can repeat positive affirmations that you are lovable over and over or that your cancer tumour will shrink. But if, as a child, you heard over and over that you were worthless and sickly, those messages programmed into your subconscious mind will undermine your best conscious efforts to change your life."

Whether you believe you can or you believe you can't, you're right.

Henry Ford

Power of belief

Just to give you a taste of how potent belief is and how it can also be used to an individual's benefit, consider the miracle of placebo medicine. There are thousands of cases of people being cured of serious disease by taking a sugar pill they believed would cure them. There are even examples of placebo surgery. Again in Lipton's book, he tells the following story . . .

In 2002, a Baylor School of Medicine study was published in the New England Journal of Medicine which demonstrated the power of the placebo effect—this time in surgery! Dr Bruce Moseley, who believed that "All good surgeons know there is no placebo effect in surgery," wanted to nevertheless assess what part of knee surgery was causing the improvement. The subjects were split into three groups. In the first, Mosley shaved the damaged cartilage in the knee. In the second, he flushed the material out of the knee which was thought to cause inflammation, and in the third, he made three standard incisions and then talked and acted as though he was doing the operation— even splashing salt water to mimic the sound of the knee-washing procedure. After 40 minutes, Moseley sewed up the incisions. All three groups were given the same aftercare and physiotherapy program.

Those who received the surgery improved as expected. What shocked Dr. Moseley to the core was that the placebo group improved by as much as the other two groups! So much so that he suggested, "My skill as a surgeon had no benefit on these patients. The entire benefit of the surgery for osteoarthritis of the knee was the placebo effect."

What you believe about yourself and your ability to create wealth plays a huge role in your results.

Perhaps you believe you're not good enough because you were told you were stupid, or perhaps you heard that your family was always cursed when it comes to money—look at what happened to Uncle Archie or Grandpa Smith, after all. Perhaps you think it's just your fate to have to struggle. Perhaps your family have always been in debt, so you don't know any different.

It doesn't matter what you were told—it matters what you believe, and if you believe it, you make it true.

Why this myth is so toxic

This is an example of a limiting belief. They are deadly to success and happiness and will lurk within your awareness for years if you don't take steps to locate and change them.

I don't care who you are or where you grew up or what school you went to or what your parents told you when you were a kid—you deserve to be financially free.

To think anything else is limiting you to a life of mediocrity. You become like the powerful elephant restrained by a length of rope tied to nothing!

The solution

None of us has time to worry about all the disparaging comments we might have heard as child! But if you feel that you may have some limiting beliefs holding you back, then seek out a professional that can help you get a new perspective.

Neuro Linguistic Programming or NLP is a great tool for quickly dismantling limiting beliefs and putting new empowering ones in their place. But there are many modalities that can help.

You could just choose a new ideal and make different decisions and choose different thoughts. Change your language and beliefs, so that when these thoughts come into our minds, we are ready with a better thought to replace them. Instead of thinking we're not worthy, decide now to do everything in your power that will make you feel good about yourself, and celebrate it with some phrase such as: "I'm a good person. I'm working hard to achieve great goals and wealth which are already coming my way!"

Catch yourself every time you hear that little voice in your head criticise what you are doing. Tell it to take a hike, and get on with creating the wealth you deserve.

New Rule of Wealth No. 21

No one deserves to be poor!

Penny Pinching Is The Way to Wealth

A miser grows rich by seeming poor. An extravagant man grows poor by seeming rich.

William Shakespeare

There are many famous misers in fiction. Perhaps the most famous of all is Charles Dickens' Ebenezer Scrooge from A Christmas Carol. Scrooge was of course portrayed as a cold-hearted, money-grabbing selfish man who cared for nothing but money. And of course it made him miserable. Dickens writes, "The cold within him froze his old features, nipped his pointed nose, made his eyes red, his thin lips blue, and he spoke out shrewdly in his grating voice . . ." Not exactly a glowing endorsement of the trait he embodied. Since the book was written in 1843, Ebenezer's last name has come into the English language as a synonym for miserliness.

There are of course countless examples of wealthy individuals who are notorious for being frugal with their money.

People like Hetty Green, an American businesswoman and the first woman to make a serious impact on Wall Street. She was regarded as the "World's Greatest Miser" in the *Guinness Book of Records* for many years, although how someone would measure that is unclear. Stories of her stinginess are legendary! She never turned on the heat nor used hot water, and is even said to have spent a night searching her house for a 2-cent stamp.

Nicknamed the "Witch of Wall Street" because of her black dresses and dishevelled look, Hetty Green died at 81 with an estimated net worth of between $100—$200 million, and that was 1916. That's between $2.4 and $4.8bn today!

The spendthrift robs his heirs; the miser robs himself.

Jean De La Bruyere

Is it in the genes?

Being considered a penny pincher is never a compliment. And it's a derogatory comment directed at whole sections of the population. The people of Yorkshire in the north of England where I have made my home are reported to be tight with money. (It's OK, I come from the south originally!) And of course the Scots have long since held the reputation of being miserly—Walt Disney's character Scrooge McDuck even talks with a Scottish accent! Interestingly, in the book, *The Millionaire Next Door*, by Thomas Stanley and William Danko, Americans with Scottish ancestry were more than five times more likely to contain millionaire households than families without Scottish roots. Perhaps the most famous of them would be Andrew Carnegie who I've mentioned several times in this book.

But there is a world of difference between being frugal, especially in the early stages of wealth creation, and being miserly.

The idea that rich people are miserable is comforting to those who have no money as they console themselves that, "well at least I spend my money and enjoy it." And certainly there seems little point working hard to accumulate vast wealth only to live like a pauper. Every few months there are stories that surface in the newspapers about some old dear who died with her 15 cats, leaving a huge fortune, to the amazement of neighbours. But to say that all wealthy people are miserable and horde away their cash is just wrong.

As I've said many times in this book, money doesn't take sides, and it doesn't cast judgement on those that have it or don't have it. It's neutral. It's only possible to make money by using money and circulating it around a financial system. Money is a means of exchange and nothing more, but the exchange or circulation is an important part of the economy, and therefore of individual wealth.

If you stuff your money under the mattress, you will actually lose money over time because of inflation. Wealthy people understand that, and instead of hoarding their money, they are far more likely to seek investments that will outstrip inflation and maintain and grow their wealth over the long term.

Be rich instead of looking rich

In the book *Millionaire Next Door*, the authors detail the findings of twenty years spent studying how people become wealthy. They note, "It is unfortunate that some people judge others by their choice in foods, beverages, suits, watches, motor vehicles and such. To them, superior people have excellent tastes in consumer goods. But it is easier to purchase products that denote superiority than to be actually superior in economic achievement. Allocating time and money in the pursuit of looking superior often has a predictable outcome: inferior economic achievement."

They go on to say, "What are three words that profile the affluent?— Frugal, Frugal, Frugal … Being frugal is the cornerstone of wealth-building."

The opposite of frugal is wasteful, and that is a one-way ticket to trouble. No one has been ruined by saving and being frugal, yet millions of people have been ruined and are being ruined by wasteful over-spending without any thought for a rainy day.

Money is like manure. You have to spread it around or it smells.

J Paul Getty

Why this myth is so toxic

Apart from the fact that it's inaccurate and misleading, this myth is damaging because it allows people who are not wealthy to feel smugly superior to those who are.

I'm not saying that if you have money, you are better than others. You are not. On the same note, however, someone with a Rolex isn't better than the person with the Timex. So if you are consoling yourself with that truth, why is it that those who don't have the money are the ones so desperate to project the image that they do? It's a contradiction.

Money doesn't make people superior, nor do the trinkets that are snapped up by the desperate—just to look the part. But money gives you freedom to buy nice things because you want to, or to save for a rainy day, or to put your kids through university. Those things are meaningful, and they are the mark of someone who has taken responsibility for their financial situation—good and bad.

The solution

Stop pretending people with money are just meaner than you, that money's not important, and that people with money should be pitied or ignored. You know you want more of the stuff, so stop sitting on the fence. Get inspired and motivated to create some real changes in your life so you can create real wealth, instead of playing at just "looking good." No one cares.

Wouldn't you rather be genuinely wealthy and wear a Timex than wear a Rolex and break out in a cold sweat every time you look at it because you can't open your credit card statements anymore?

New Rule of Wealth No. 22
You have to be wise with your money if you want to be rich.

It's Rude To Talk About Money!

Your own words are the bricks and mortar of the dreams you want to realize.
Your words are the greatest power you have. The words you choose and use establish
the life you experience.

Sonia Croquette

Says who? I've never understood this myth. OK, no one likes to listen to someone bragging about how much money they make or how big their bonus was this year, or even how much debt they have (and how they can't sleep at night)—but talking about money isn't rude.

According to Bill Bryson in his book *Mother Tongue,* the revised Oxford English Dictionary has 615,000 words. If you add technical and medical words, the tally reaches into the millions. It is estimated, however, that there are only 200,000 English words in common use, yet the average person's vocabulary is between 2,000 and 10,000 words.

EXCUSE ME SIR, I DON'T MEAN TO BE RUDE, BUT IT SEEMS THAT YOUR STOCK QUOTATION HAS JUST CRASHED!

Language is vital

The simple fact of the matter is that a lack of vocabulary limits your ability to understand and appreciate certain topics. Words are the building blocks of thought. They allow us to express ideas and describe new experiences. It is not rude to talk about money. On the contrary, it is essential to talk about money.

If you are a vet, you need to understand animal anatomy in order to diagnose and heal a patient, the same with medical doctors. How confident would you feel if you went to your local GP and told him of your conditions and he said, "Mmm yes, not sure about that, but I think you're thingy (pointing to somewhere in your stomach) might be blocked up." If, on the other hand, he tells you that your small intestine is causing you trouble and it's easily treated, your faith is restored.

We need language to communicate ideas. We need words to express learning and build knowledge. If, therefore, you never talk about money because you think it's rude, then you will be as familiar with it as you are with the digestive system of a sheep. If you don't know anything about money, and you never discuss it, then how can you possibly work out how to make it and keep it?

Without the words to describe something, that thing can't exist! Native American languages have no word for "lie." It is a concept that is totally unfamiliar with the people, and as such, is not part of their thinking, their behaviour or their language. Lying doesn't exist in their culture. The Tasaday tribe in the Philippines reportedly has no words to describe "dislike," "hate" or "war," and these things don't exist in their world either. Without words to describe a concept, it doesn't seem to exist. And without a concept existing, neither does the language.

Bryson tells us that residents of the Trobriand Islands in Papua, New Guinea, have 100 words for yams, while the Maoris of New Zealand have 35 words for dung, and apparently the Arabs are said to have 6,000 words for camels and camel equipment!

Words form the thread on which we string our experience.

Alduos Huxley

If you don't talk about it, you can't understand it

We may not need that level of specificity, but a lack of financial vocabulary hinders your experience of money. If you don't have any knowledge of financial language and can't talk coherently and knowledgeably about money, then chances are you won't have any in your life. It's that simple.

If you want to make money in property development, for example, you have to understand the lingo. Being able to confidently converse in all aspects of that industry is part of the investment. You have to understand the jargon and specific industry terms, otherwise you are much more likely to make an error in negotiations or in some part of the investment.

The same is true of investing in the stock market. If you want to know about the companies you are going to invest in, you have to understand things like PE ratios and what constitutes a good one and a bad one. There is no merit in relying on other people all the time.

Warren Buffett, a man who knows a thing or two about wealth, says that if you want to create wealth, "You should have knowledge of how business operates and the language of business, some enthusiasm for the subject and qualities of temperament which may be more important than IQ points. These will enable you to think independently and to avoid various forms of mass hysteria that infect the investment makers from time to time."

If you are sceptical about the importance of the language you use and the power it has over your thoughts and outcomes, try out the following experiment:

Pair up with a friend—one of you is A, the other is B. Person A is to hold their arm straight out to the side. Person B is to try and push A's arm down at the wrist and B is to resist as much as possible. This will gauge the baseline strength.

Take a moment and relax. Person A is to repeat out loud the phrase, "I am weak" 20 times and put their arm out in the same way as before. Now person A is to push down at the wrist.

Take a moment again and repeat the exercise with the phrase, "I am strong." Nine times out of ten there is a marked difference in strength between the "weak" and "strong" sessions, and it's just a simple demonstration of the power of language.

We invent the world through language. The world occurs through language.

Mal Pancoast

Why this myth is so toxic

If you believe this myth, and you therefore don't want to be rude, you will never discuss money. It will become a topic that is not suitable for "polite company," and as such, you will never truly understand money. If you can't understand a topic, how can you ever master it?

This myth, therefore, stops you gaining any form of financial literacy.

The solution

Buy a basic economics book or borrow one from your library so that you can understand the basic terms that govern money. It is, for example, frightening that the vast majority of people have no idea what rate of interest they are paying on their credit card.

Seek initially to understand the basics. Listen to financial programmes on the TV and see if you can understand what is being discussed. If you don't, then hop online or visit the library until you do. Get used to talking about money and financial issues.

New Rule of Wealth No. 23

It is financial suicide NOT to talk about money.

Myth

24

Getting Wealthy Is A Win/ Lose Game

*Let's face it. In most of life we really are interdependent. We need each other.
Staunch independence is an illusion, but heavy dependence isn't healthy, either.
The only position of long-term strength is interdependence: win/win.*

Greg Anderson

People who believe this myth usually believe that to make money one has to make some sort of Faustian pact, whereby in return for wealth all else must be surrendered: happiness, friends, family, leisure, interests . . . even principles.

Deal with the devil

Faust is the protagonist of a classic German legend who makes a deal with the devil in exchange for knowledge. The interpretation has changed over the ages, and Faust has taken on a slightly different meaning to describe someone whose headstrong desire for wealth and self-fulfilment leads them in dangerous moral directions. Consequently, this myth is closely related to myths 4 and 13, which discuss greed and corruption.

In addition, there is an assumption that for someone to win, someone else must lose. This is especially relevant to business, and on the surface, it's hard to argue with the perspective.

If you look at some of the global labels that have got into hot water over the years for moving manufacturing to developing regions, it's hard to imagine that the workers who are essentially paid a pittance aren't losers in that game. Especially when their entire annual salary wouldn't allow them to buy one pair of the trainers or jeans they were making. Sadly, the drive for shareholder benefit has resulted in too many business decisions being made where the shareholders win and the workers lose.

But it isn't always that way.

For every example of business that is exploiting natural resources or local workforces, there are umpteen other examples of companies sharing their wealth and doing extremely well. Only it's not nearly as interesting and newsworthy as the horror stories of child labour. As a result, you rarely hear about it.

Money is always there, but the pockets change.

Gertrude Stein

Win/win

One of the most famous "good guy" examples is when US company International Harvester was in serious financial trouble. It was suggested that the staff at the Springfield plant buy their part of the business, and Jack Stack and twelve managers jumped at the chance. In February 1983, they took over—with no money, no resources and 119 people all depending on them to save their jobs.

Stack was a sports enthusiast, and because of the challenges facing the company, they didn't have time for restructuring or endless meetings. He believed in one foundation principal—you get what you give! And instead of the usual game of win/lose business, he created what would come to be known as *The Great Game of Business*. At the heart of the Game is a very simple proposition: "The best, most efficient, most profitable way to operate a business is to give everybody in the company a voice in saying how the company is run and a stake in the financial outcome, good or bad."

From 1983 to 1986, sales grew more than 30% per year, going from a loss of $60,488 in the first year to pre-tax earnings of $2.7m four years later. Even when they lost a contract representing 40% of their business, there were no lay-offs. No one lost.

SRC is now a collection of 22 separate companies with combined revenue over $120m. Many of those new businesses have come from employees spotting opportunities or ways to improve performance. *The Great Game of Business* and the philosophy of open book management have since been successfully adopted by other businesses. SRC created "Go-givers" not Go-getters; they were not interested in a win/lose mentality, only win/win and collective success. And it worked.

The best way to strive for wealth, or anything else for that matter, is through a balanced approach in which all of our physical and emotional needs are met. There can be fewer more rewarding things in the world than to pursue something meaningful that will help more than just you and your family, whilst also finding time for the people we value in our lives. That is the best way to achieve success in all our efforts and goals.

Of course, there are examples of people who gave up everything to acquire wealth and became wealthy. But they also lost the relationships that mattered along the way, most of all with themselves. They became cold, friendless and lost the joy of being somewhere en route. To become obsessed with creating wealth is a kind of madness. In that madness, there is usually a loser, and it's not the person you imagine. There is nothing pleasurable about selling out to achieve wealth.

Have you ever seen the movie *Family Man* with Nicholas Cage and Téa Leoni? Cage's character is a fast-lane investment broker who gets the opportunity to go back and see how his life would have turned out had he not made certain decisions. He is mortified to wake up to a wife and family in the suburbs. To start with he is devastated, but then when he finally goes back to his old life he realises how empty and lonely it is. The money he so craved didn't make him happy at all. He missed the warmth and laughter of his family.

The darkest day of any man's life is when he sits down to plan how to get money without earning it.

Horace Greeley

Why this myth is so toxic

Most people don't want to go out of their way to make someone unhappy. Most people don't like the idea that their gain will automatically be someone else's loss. Even if we don't know that person, there are moral standards that we live by, and making someone else miserable is not usually on the top of the "must do today" list. Consequently, if you genuinely believe this myth, then why on earth would you put yourself out there to make money?

If you think that your making money is going to take it out of someone else's pocket, you are unlikely to want to do what needs to be done.

But it doesn't have to be that way. A good business helps everyone along the supply chain, from the producers of the raw materials, their families, all the way through manufacture and into the hands of the consumer. If everyone takes a little slice—everyone wins.

The solution

Instead of seeing money as a win/lose game, change your way of thinking to play a win/win game. It is possible. You can choose where you invest your money and who you invest it with. You therefore have an opportunity to vote for win/win with your investment money.

The old way of working is hopefully dying off, and we are going to need to find ways of helping others. In that process we will help ourselves and those we care about.

To be enthused and excited by what wealth can achieve for you and others is a much healthier option.

You have everything to lose if you do nothing. You also have everything to gain, if you want it enough!

New Rule of Wealth No. 24

You don't need to use dirty tricks to be filthy rich!

Money Is Power

Money, or even power, can never yield happiness unless it is accompanied by the goodwill of others.

B.C. Forbes

On the face of it, there seems to be a connection between money and power. Those with money are able to jump waiting lists and buy private health care; they may be better treated by business owners keen to keep their custom. They can demand more than those without money because they have money.

Business common sense

But is that really power, or just pleasant? From the businesses' viewpoint, isn't it just common sense? If you owned a restaurant and someone wealthy wanted a table, isn't it only smart business to make sure that person is given the best table and the best waiter? He is, after all, most likely to order an expensive meal and tip handsomely. Plus, if he's happy, he'll come back and may bring some rich friends! If you were a travel agent, would you bend over backwards to accommodate the requests and requirements of your millionaire clients, or would you bump them for a family of four that wants seven nights in Benidorm?

Much of the power that is associated with money is simple business acumen. It's self-interest. The wealthy live a different life than most people, especially those who have inherited wealth. They simply don't think the same way. To them, money is a free pass, an access-all-areas invitation to the very best the world has to offer. And anyone who provides those things would be a fool not to tap in to that wealth.

But to say that having money automatically gives you power is a myth. Power is power, and it comes from a whole host of places. Money is only one of them.

So in that respect, like so many of the myths we have covered (and uncovered) in this book, money is just part of the puzzle.

You may have power if you have intelligence and are well-educated—whether that comes from formal education or a voracious appetite for books. That knowledge gives you power too.

When you understand something or broaden your experiences, you gain wisdom, which gives you power. Money is not the only way, therefore, to secure power. If you use that knowledge to take action then you have even greater power.

There are also those who have power and don't necessarily have money. Take critics for example—be that film, book, food or any other sort. Some of these individuals wield huge power—enough to finish a career or close a restaurant. Are they rich? Usually not! But they are powerful.

Other examples of people with plenty of power without necessarily buckets of cash are politicians. The huge expenses scandal which happened in the UK shortly before this book was published, and which saw politicians individually claim huge sums of taxpayer money on spurious grounds, certainly doesn't do much to dispel the myths about money and greed. However, politicians' power comes from the influence they can bring to bear, not the money they squirrel out the system.

To say money is power is only part of the equation.

There are two fools in this world. One is the millionaire who thinks that by hoarding money he can somehow accumulate real power, and the other is the penniless reformer who thinks that if only he can take the money from one class and give it to another, all the world's ills will be cured.

Henry Ford

Power is influence

Power comes from influence and choice. Everyone wants to feel a sense of control over their own life. Everyone wants to feel a sense of fulfilment and as though what they do matters. We all want to feel loved and cared for and enjoy time to relax with friends and family. Money allows us those things because it removes a baseline worry that pollutes so many lives.

According to the May 2009 figures of Credit Action, a UK debt counselling and management charity set up to help people "avoid the pain of debt," a recent poll conducted by the Resolution Foundation found that nearly three million Britons now worry "all the time" about their personal finances. This is double the number found in 2007. Almost six million fear their homes will be repossessed, according to research from *Which?*, the independent consumer protection organisation. Homeowners are feeling the pinch with 62% of the UK's working population fretful that they or their partner may lose their job, and over four in ten (43%) joint-income households are anxious that they wouldn't be able to pay their mortgage. And this is just the picture in my country. Doubtless, the global statistics paint a very similar picture.

Being constantly worried about money is extremely disempowering and causes all sorts of additional challenges, including health problems and ongoing stress.

Having money gives us choices that we wouldn't have otherwise. And that's where its real power comes from.

Enthusiasm is the greatest asset in the world. It beats money, power and influence.

Henry Chester

Why this myth is so toxic

There is something distasteful about this myth. There is an assumption of greed or corruption, and that money in some way pollutes the soul. Nothing could be further from the truth. Money has the potential to liberate the soul to pursue the things that will make you happy. If you dream of being a dancer or an artist, but you have no money, then you will never have the freedom to pursue those desires. Living costs money. There are bills to pay and mouths to feed, and that constant demand for cash often keeps us bound to a path that is not fulfilling us on a deep personal level.

Having money doesn't make you powerful, but it gives you choices and that, in itself, gives you power. If you knew that you could not fail, what would you be doing right now? Would you still go to work tomorrow, or would you completely change your life? Would your today be different from your yesterday?

The solution

Just to set the record straight, money won't magically eradicate all your problems. But it does eradicate a lot of them. You will have new types of problems, such as worrying about where to invest your money for the best return, or how to deal with requests from friends and family for 'loans,' but that's got to be a better sort of concern than how you are going to eat this month!

You have to stop thinking of money as possessing traits and characteristics. It will not give you power or make you greedy or any of the other myths that assume that money makes you a worse person.

Money can make you a happier person by giving you a degree of freedom and choice. That is its power. Power to take responsibility for your life. Power to choose how you spend your time and who you spend it with. Power to pursue gifts and talents and enjoy the very best life has to offer.

Power over others is one thing, power with and through others is quite another.

New Rule of Wealth No. 25

Great wealth requires great responsibility.

The Rich Are Not Humble

To be humble to superiors is duty, to equals courtesy, to inferiors nobleness.

Benjamin Franklin

Like so many of these myths, this one tries to give money a personality. As ever, it's a negative one too. But money is money, and the personality belongs to the people who have it or don't have it.

This myth is therefore as accurate as assuming everyone with money is greedy or corrupt, and that everyone who is poor is honest and hard-working. It's rubbish—absolute rubbish!

It was created by pious individuals who like to stand on their moral high-ground and talk of all the virtues of poverty—and how having nothing somehow made you, by definition, a better or stronger person. How can that be true?

Just think about it for a moment. Think of the least humble person you know . . . Does that person have money?

In the fabric of gratitude are woven the threads of humility.

Steven Vitrano

Humility is not dependant on money

For me, I know several extremely rich people who I wouldn't want to share a meal with because they are so full of themselves. All they want to do is talk about themselves and find ways to pat themselves on the back and expect you to do the same all the time. These individuals wouldn't know how to spell humility, never mind exercise it.

But I also know rich people who you would never even guess were wealthy. They are grateful for all they have and are happy to share their time and expertise. There is an ordinariness about them, and that's what makes them attractive. They rarely talk business in social situations and are always more interested in what I'm doing than crowing about their bank accounts or the deal they have just been involved in.

If you need an example of how erroneous this myth is, look no further than Warren Buffet. Known as the "Oracle of Omaha," Buffet is one of the most successful investors of all time, and is at the time of writing estimated to be worth in excess of $37bn. Yet he still lives in the same house in the central Dundee neighbourhood of Omaha that he bought in 1958 for $31,500. He does own a $4 million home in Laguna Beach California, but that's hardly extravagant, considering his wealth.

Buffet is reported to still eat at the local diner and still drives the same Crown Victoria car, and his favourite drink is Cherry Cola. When Buffet did splash out on a private jet, he sheepishly called it the "*The Indefensible.*"

None of these things sit comfortably with the idea that wealthy people are not humble. You'll be doing well to get wealthier than Warren Buffet (he's second only to Bill Gates in wealth) and yet he is, by all accounts, the personification of humility.

At the other end of the wealth scale, I know some people who have very little money, but who aren't humble either. Instead, they curse their fate, blaming everyone from their family to the government for their financial situation. It's never their own fault.

I even know a few introverted snobs who bang on about their "humble" roots and how hard it was for them. They wear their financial poverty like a brightly-ribboned medal as though it indicates some moral superiority!

There is nothing humble or arrogant about money. It's just a reflection of the person who is holding that money.

Early in life, I had to choose between honest arrogance and hypocritical humility. I chose honest arrogance and have seen no occasions to change.

Frank Lloyd Wright

Perception is projection

Noted Swiss psychiatrist, Carl Jung, stated that "perception is projection." In other words, what we perceive to be true is nothing more than a projection of our own internal opinions, ideas and beliefs. We interpret the outside world to mean whatever we believe on the inside. The world as we see it is therefore nothing but a mirror to our own selves.

If someone is angry and bitter or sees the arrogance in everyone they meet, then those are the filters through which they view the world. As a result, they meet angry, bitter and arrogant people and have their perspective validated. Their experiences of life are therefore dominated by those traits. Perhaps Napoleon Hill says it best in his book *Think and Grow Rich* where he references an un-named philosopher who says, *"It was a great surprise to me when I discovered that most of the ugliness I saw in others, was but a reflection of my own nature."*

Why this myth is so toxic

If you believe this myth, then you fail to take action toward wealth because you fear it will make you arrogant. But you and I both know that is rubbish, and that this myth is just used to comfort those who dream of great wealth, but are not prepared to do anything other than buy their scratch cards to make it happen.

It is a way to dress up the truth—your envy of wealth. What is the point of blaming others who have more money than you for real or imaginary shortcomings? Who cares if they are humble or not humble? Making sweeping generalisations, even if we believe them to be true, is simply a trick to sabotage your own progress.

What matters is what you are doing. You can't control what others do; you can't control whether money makes them a better person or a worse person. But you can control how it impacts you and your loved ones.

The solution

If you want wealth, and envy those with money, then resolve to join their ranks. That isn't going to happen by accident.

Concentrate on your own desires and take personal responsibility for financial fate. Stop judging and whingeing! It's time to show how good YOU are. You are the only competition that matters.

Take a stand, create the wealth you dream of and be a shining example of all the good that wealth can be and create.

New Rule of Wealth No. 26

Money acts as a mirror, reflecting you as you really are.

The Rich Get Richer And The Poor Get Poorer

I don't think of myself as a poor deprived ghetto girl who made good. I think of myself as somebody who from an early age knew I was responsible for myself, and I had to make good.

Oprah Winfrey

This is the myth of headlines, the one you always think of when a new story emerges about the poverty of a developing country. We "tut-tut" at the TV and mentally chastise the rich for making the poor poorer. It is the catch-cry against capitalism because it discusses economic equality.

Like myth #1, it may have its roots in the Bible . . .

"For whosoever hath, to him shall be given, and he shall have more abundance: but whosoever hath not, from him shall be taken away even that he hath."

Only like myth #1, it was taken out of context. In this verse, Jesus is not referring to economic inequality, but is replying to the question, "Why speakest thou unto them in parables?" Jesus says his parables give fresh understanding only to those who already have accepted his message.

This myth is also closely related to myth #24 which assumes that for someone to become rich, someone else must become poor—that money is finite. The rich hang on to it or find ways to multiply that wealth. For the poor, however, money slips through their fingers like sand.

There is certainly no shortage of evidence that this myth is true. It's been a subject of debate and political discussion for centuries.

Andrew Jackson, the 7ᵗʰ President of the United States, said in his 1832 bank veto that "when the laws undertake . . . to make the rich richer and the potent more powerful, the humble members of society . . . have a right to complain of the injustice to their Government."

Useful advice, and certainly something that might have helped avert the financial crisis the US now faces over 150 years later.

But is it really true?

Successful people make money. It's not that people who make money become successful, but that successful people attract money. They bring success to what they do.

Wayne Dyer

The poor are getting richer

One report that is widely cited as proof for this theory is the *1999 United Nations Human Development Report* which stated: "Gaps in income between the poorest and richest countries have continued to widen. In 1960, the 20% of the world's people in the richest countries had 30 times the income of the poorest 20% — in 1997, 74 times as much." It added that "gaps are widening both between and within countries."

However, according to Xavier Sala-i-Martin, an economist at Columbia University, the numbers used to arrive at this conclusion were misleading. Some of the analysis had departed from standard economic procedures, like not correcting for price levels from country to country. The biggest problem with the data, however, was that it looked at gaps in income between rich and poor countries, not rich and poor individuals.

If you consider, for example, that the economies of the world's two most populous countries, China and India, have raced ahead over the last 30 years, this results in 2.5 billion poorer people becoming richer—thus decreasing global poverty and increasing equality.

In Sala-i-Martin's paper, "The Disturbing `Rise' of Global Income Inequality," he focuses on people, not countries, and the results are striking.

The rich did get richer faster than the poor did. But for the most part, the poor did not get poorer. They got richer too. Sala-i-Martin says, "One would like to think that it is unambiguously good that more than a third of the poorest citizens see their incomes grow and converge to the levels enjoyed by the richest people in the world. And if our indexes say that inequality rises, then rising inequality must be good, and we should not worry about it!"

Grameen Bank

One man who has done a great deal to help the poor become richer is Muhammad Yunus, founder of the Grameen Bank. He says, "I did something that challenged the banking world. Conventional banks look for the rich; we look for the absolutely poor. All people are entrepreneurs, but many don't have the opportunity to find out."

The Grameen Bank gives people that opportunity. Yunus and the Grameen Bank were awarded the Nobel Peace Prize in 2006, "for efforts to create economic and social development from below." Since inception, this successful micro-finance model has inspired similar efforts in hundreds of countries in the developing world, allowing the poor to become richer.

———

There's nothing wrong with wanting to make money—except that it should not become the sole objective. The end should be to provide a service or produce a product.

William M. Batten, former CEO of J.C. Penney

Why this myth is so toxic

The idea that one person's wealth is another's poverty is damaging for the same reason that the rest of the myths are damaging. It is designed to make those without money feel better about their situation. Whereas the only thing that would really make them feel better is a change of situation.

If you don't have money, then YOU can change that. Regardless of what you have done in the past or whether you lunge from one financial crisis to the next—if you want to change it, you can.

Your building wealth does not take food from the babes of the poor. If anything, it offers a greater chance for the money to circulate and do even more good. In a modern economic society, many "poor" people do have a certain level of income, but they often spend much of it on things that don't multiply their income. Have you noticed that many "poor" people—certainly those who would be categorised as such by studies on poverty—always seem to find the money for a beer, or a packet of cigarettes, or a bet? And they may even watch to see if their lottery numbers come up on their large-screen digital televisions.

The solution

The solution is not the double roll-over or the Jackpot. The UK lottery is marketed with the slogan "It Could Be You", but the mocking T-shirt they tried to ban is more realistic: "It Won't Be You". You are the only person that can make you rich. You have to want it badly enough that you will make those little sacrifices.

In the end, you have to find a big enough "why" for yourself. You have to work out what you really want, and whether or not it's important enough for you. Viktor Frankl, who survived the Nazi concentration camps and went on to become a well-respected psychiatrist, once said, "Those who have a 'why' to live, can bear almost any 'how.'"

You have to decide if becoming financially free is important enough for you. If you find a big enough "why," then you will take the ideas in this book to the streets and make it happen. Otherwise, you might just take a trip back to the book store and look for the next book on wealth. In fact I can recommend a good one . . .

The choice is yours.

New Rule of Wealth No. 27

Wealth is in constant circulation.

Make changes, make money

I trust reading this book has helped you to understand better some of the attitudes and circumstances that may have been holding you back from wealth-creation.

I hope too that it has pointed you in the direction of what you can do about it. I said at the outset that this book is not really about money, but about you, and for this book to really make a difference to your life, you will have to change in some significant but positive ways. No problem there. Change is always possible, and is often most effective when you start with a good model. Your model should be those who have already done it.

During the course of their investigations into wealthy households, the authors of *The Millionaire Next Door* discovered seven common denominators amongst those who successfully built wealth;

1. They lived well below their means.
2. They allocated their time, energy and money efficiently in ways conducive to building wealth.
3. They believed that financial independence is more important than displaying high social status.
4. Their parents did not provide economic outpatient care.
5. Their adult children were economically self-sufficient.
6. They were proficient in targeting market opportunities.
7. They chose the right occupation.

There is nothing mysterious about the similar traits in the success of these individuals. Making money is all about making it a priority and taking the necessary steps to put yourself in a position where you can create wealth, grow it and keep it.

That's not always going to be easy, especially if you are up to your neck in debt, but it is always possible, and it is never too late to start.

And the 27 money myths? The point is, you never will get started as long as you are saddled with their psychological and emotional baggage. Most of these myths portray money in a bad light. Those discussed here, and perhaps some of your own myths that you highlighted at the start of the book, constitute your own personal "reign of error" when it comes to our relationship with money.

They form a roof on your aspirations and actions and stop you from taking the necessary steps toward financial freedom.

So remember, and believe. Money is not the root of all evil, and it doesn't take sides. It doesn't corrupt, and people don't always have to lose. It won't turn you into a miser or a greedy monster. It will not make you an absentee parent or a poor friend. Money won't miraculously solve all your problems, but it can help you to solve them in style!

Money gives you more options—options to choose how to spend your days, freedom to pursue hobbies and interests unencumbered by financial concerns, freedom to spend time with those you love, freedom to enjoy the very best life has to offer. It's up to you. Experience it, nothing wavering. Forget luck. Get to work. Start to change. And I promise you, with more sincerity than any lottery-ticket seller ever will . . . truly, it could be you.